The
Philosophy
of
Gardening

The Philosophy of Gardening

edited by Blanka Stolz
translated by Karen Caruana

Invisible Publishing
Halifax & Prince Edward County

First published in 2017 as *Die Philosophie des Gartnerns* by Mairisch Verlag, Hamburg, Germany | Translation © Karen Caruana, 2021

Library and Archives Canada Cataloguing in Publication

Title: The philosophy of gardening / edited by Blanka Stolz ;
    translated by Karen Caruana.

Other titles: Philosophie des Gärtnerns. English

Names: Stolz, Blanka, editor. | Caruana, Karen, translator.

Identifiers: Canadiana (print) 20210169400
    Canadiana (ebook) 20210169532

ISBN 9781988784694 (softcover) | ISBN 9781988784762 (HTML)

Subjects: LCSH: Gardening—Philosophy.

Classification: LCC SB454.3.P45 P4513 2021 | DDC 635.01—dc23

Cover and interior design by Megan Fildes | Typeset in Laurentian
With thanks to type designer Rod McDonald

Printed and bound in Canada
Invisible Publishing | Halifax & Prince Edward County
www.invisiblepublishing.com

Published with the generous assistance of the Canada Council for the Arts, the Ontario Arts Council, and the Government of Canada. The translation of this work was supported by a grant from the Goethe-Institut.

KAREN CARUANA

Translator's Note

I began this translation in late March 2020. The effects of the pandemic lockdown were beginning to make themselves felt. Not much later, at least here in Ontario's plant hardiness zone 6, the planting season began. Like many well-intentioned part-time gardeners also juggling full-time freelance work, family life, and, in my case, a flock of twenty or so chickens, four goats, two dogs, three cats, and a rabbit, I didn't get my seeds started on time, so near the end of May I found myself scrambling to find seed packets and seedlings at our local farmers' markets and garden centres. Unbeknownst to me, the pandemic had not just unleashed a wave of DIY home renovation projects among bored, socially isolated home-owners (causing a lumber shortage—imagine!), it had also awoken a need to feel a sense of control, self-sufficiency. I was affected even more by the seedling shortage because I had, during the mid-winter seed catalogue perusing season, when garden enthusiasts envision the perfect garden, resplendent with brightly coloured flowers and perfectly weeded rows of vegetables, resisted the urge to order more seeds, choosing instead to use up the seeds in my stash. Whether your hobby is gardening, knitting, sewing, woodworking, or making jewellery, I'm sure you've experienced the guilty pleasure of spontaneously increasing your collection of "someday I'll use this..." items. Unfortunately, I discovered that many of the seeds in my stash had lost their power to germinate. Having operated a certified organic herb and vegetable farm for years (following an escape from Toronto in 2004), I was quite confident in my seed-planting abilities, and I knew this was not a user error.

And so translating this book became a consolation of sorts. I could garden vicariously through the texts I was translating. The pieces in this book cover a range of topics, and I found myself caught up not just in finding the best phrase to do justice to the original German, but also pondering my own relationship with gardening.

Starting with the bigger, metaphysical picture, where does my garden begin? Does it begin with the lawn around our home, forming a boundary between our (somewhat) structured life and the unruliness of nature? At one time, when we lived in Toronto, we saw our xeriscaped, naturalized garden as a way of keeping the concrete jungle at bay. But now we live on one hundred acres, so the lawn around our house acts as a barrier of sorts between ourselves and the surrounding woods, and whatever is lurking there. This includes unwelcome, intrusive pests, like ticks and mosquitoes and blackflies, which are less able to propagate in a mowed lawn.

The act of planting seeds is more of a detail-oriented task, done on a much smaller scale than sitting on a lawn tractor. I found myself wondering if I was tolerant of the self-seeded "volunteers" in my vegetable garden. Considering the random scattering of sunflower plants throughout my vegetable bed (thank you, chickadees) and my joy at finding early spring lettuce reseeded from the plants I'd allowed to bolt the summer before, I'd say yes. Does this make me more tolerant and benevolent to the differences of others? I'd like to think so.

Speaking of vegetable gardens, to what extent is gardening a way to control nature? To be able to enjoy the bounty of my vegetable garden, the weeds have to be kept under control. This past spring, I adopted a "work smarter, not harder" approach and let go of the tidily maintained rows of vegetables of my German youth and mulched the entire garden with hay. The result? A bounty of potatoes in a drought-plagued summer, where others had only paltry crops. Fewer hours spent weeding and watering. And less work meant less resentment toward my "hobby," a moniker I began to question while translating one of the pieces that discusses the role gender plays in gardening. Was I keeping a garden because of my sense of obligation as a caregiver, or is it an activity I enjoy filling my limited leisure time with? Or do I simply need a more tangible sense of achievement when I'm not at my computer marvelling at the process of the words broadcast by my brain being sown in tidy rows across my screen?

Translation is a bit like gardening. It is a lengthy, gradual process. It involves weeding out words and expressions that don't quite fit. It's about creating an arrangement of words that fit into the landscape of the text. Like a plant that doesn't flourish in different surroundings, sometimes a turn of phrase needs careful attention so that its translation suits its new language environment. It is a solitary task, just as gardening quite often is. While gardening can be done in the company of others, only one set of hands can place a tiny seed in the earth. You plant the seed, and then you step back and let the seed do its thing. You return later to nurture it, whether through watering, or weeding, or pruning. Translation is much the same. Translate. Let it sit. Come back to it, weed out the words that don't fit, prune out the unnecessary tangents that bear no fruit, nurture the text by carefully massaging it until you get it right. And even then, the expert eyes of a good editor are invaluable (thank you, Leigh). Like gardening, translation is a learning process. Just as a gardener is not born with a green thumb, growing up speaking more than one language does not make you a translator. Gardening is something you learn by doing, an experience lived, lessons learned. The art of translation is also not learned overnight. It requires living the language, not just the one you are translating from. And it is also extremely helpful to have experience in the subject matter.

As I write this, eleven months have passed since I began this translation. It is not yet too late for me to order seeds, to connect with local growers for seedlings, to dream of my vision of the perfect garden. This vision does not include impeccably weeded rows of vegetables, nor the expectation that every seedling must have been started by yours truly. But it does include taking the time to enjoy a good book outdoors, in the garden. Once mosquito and blackfly season has passed, of course.

Wishing you a perfect gardening season.

Karen Caruana has been practising the craft of translation for over fifteen years now, working from German and French into English. When not mulling over words, she is an avid gardener (she once operated an organic herb farm), a passionate environmentalist, teaches yoga, and enjoys spending time outdoors. She lives in Marmora, Ontario.

I'm in the Garden—In Lieu of a Foreword

"The garden—which is an order of the human soul and related to all its other orders—is an order of the whole soul and not of any half of it. It can never belong to only the active and not to the indolent half of the soul. And there are no self-righteous aesthetes, if not for strollers, to whom it offers no reproach. The garden must have its gardener."[1]

I'm in the gardens at Munt la Reita, a farm located in the mountains of Ticino.[2] It might be May, but it's still very cold and feels like winter. The garden has been mulched with hay; the branches of the red currant shrubs have been tied together so they can bear the weight of the snow without snapping. There is nary a green thing in sight; only the rhubarb is holding its own. Everything else is varying shades of brown. I can't help but think there is no way this garden will ever be green again, lush and overgrown, resplendent with brightly coloured flowers. I wonder how others can place their faith in nature's cycles. What is it that, year after year, drives a philosophizing gardener, or a gardening philosopher, to once again pick up a shovel and a rake and get back into the garden?

This question is central to gardening, and is one the authors in this book also wrestle with. In doing so, they contemplate not only the philosophical, but also the historical, sociological, cultural, and political aspects of gardens and gardening.

When you stand in a kitchen garden, the first and most

obvious answer to the question of why you go to all the effort is self-sufficiency, to satiate the belly and the spirit. This leads directly to the next questions: What to plant, and how much? Which seed varieties to choose? In her essay "Planting, Saving, and Propagating Heirloom Vegetables," Annette Holländer examines the question of which plants we should grow, their qualities—flavour, robustness, seed stability—and the joy that can be derived from growing special varieties in your own garden and eating them. But what will grow in a garden at 1,400 metres above sea level, and what things are not even worth planting? Verena Senn, who, with her husband, Markus, has been maintaining the Munt la Reita organic garden for thirty years, knows which plants are worth their time, and which aren't.

As for me, I still don't have enough faith in the ability of the sun, heat, and water to make the plants sprout. We stand there together in the fog and try to sketch out the future beds and paths, to come up with a plan. We're doing what gardeners have always done: determining what will be planted where, using beds, paths, hedges, and shrubs to create a boundary between *untamed nature* and cultivated garden. It is our creative drive that defines a garden. In his essay "On the Metaphysics of a Garden," Dieter Wandschneider goes one step further by following in the footsteps of Kant and Hegel. He writes that it is the tension between natural and artistic design that differentiates a garden from nature, and from cultivated natural forms such as fields, meadows, and forests. Therefore, a garden is design imposed on nature.

Sarah Thelen, in her contribution "Leaves That Mean the World," is also of the opinion that a garden is something between an artificial construct and a living, natural entity. And yet in the end, a garden does what it wants, according to Thelen. It changes constantly, outgrows itself, is unpredictable, blossoms—and the gardener has to constantly redefine their position in relation to it.

Another factor the gardener cannot influence is the weather. Its impact starts well before the harvest season, as early as when it is time to plant seeds. The weather forecast determines the planting days in May, and Maria Thun notes the work to be done in the garden on her calendar.[3] It seems as though it always rains heavily on root days—the days when potatoes, celery root, and radishes are to be planted. I spend hours kneeling in the dry greenhouse, weeding. A week later, the rain subsides and it is a root day: the first hundred seed potatoes are dropped into the ground, the first onions are planted, and two rows of carrots are sown. We cover the potatoes with compost and a thick layer of mulch consisting of goat manure and hay. The soil is protected from the wind and the sun by the layer of hay and will not dry out so quickly; it also reduces weed growth and keeps away snails. With every layer we place over the plants, I find myself hoping we're doing the right thing.

Doing the right thing. That age-old yearning to live a good life, a theme woven into the history of philosophy since the time of Aristotle, is one that resonates when considering the motivation behind gardening. Does cultivating land, planting and caring for plants—gardening—transform you into a better, more virtuous person? In the Munt la Reita garden, horticultural faith is put to the test in the month of May: the farm is hit with another snowfall. Their summers—and here, summer means the period when temperature and sunlight are sufficient to allow plants to grow at its higher altitude—are short, shorter than in the lowlands, so they can't afford to delay their planting by much. We are consumed by the feeling that time is running out because we've had to put planting on hold. Fortunately, we are blessed by a brief intermezzo and the snow quickly melts. We prepare the rows and raised beds and begin to transplant the cabbage, kohlrabi, and Swiss chard seedlings that were started in the greenhouse.

Working in a garden seems to induce a sense of meditative calm, a mindset that's been described as desirable by philosophers from Epicurus to Hume. Compared to the digital world, where we can explore our environment without bending over, gardening requires physical activity. But the reason urban green spaces and gardens are making a comeback among office workers is due to a desire for more physical activity—today's gardeners are even seen as athletes.[4]

Let's look back a generation: in her piece "Gardening in Tune with Nature," Elke von Radziewsky discusses Rob Leopold, who saw himself as the first independent garden philosopher, and whose practical gardening philosophy shaped the 1980s gardening movement in the Netherlands. He and his supporters, who were true garden individualists, were concerned with the naturalness of a garden. They saw the garden as a place where people understand nature, something to monitor with a sense of wonder and an inquiring mind.

Nowadays, organic fruit and vegetables can be found at markets and in supermarkets; growing your own isn't necessarily cheaper. Gardening is no longer a necessity. And yet the current DIY enthusiasm, the quest to work with nature by customizing available shapes and surfaces—whether in the city, in the suburbs, or in the country—seems to be the driving force behind the next generation of gardeners.[5] Their gardens no longer look like the ones in a hardware store flier: lawns and conifers have given way to fruit trees, homemade raised beds, and naturalized hedgerows. In these intergenerational gardens, intercultural gardens, neighbourhood and community gardens, but also in cultivated, formerly fallow urban spaces, it appears that something else is growing through gardening, in addition to the plants: long-lost fellowship, meaningfulness, and mindfulness. Even if, in some locations, the urban garden has become the project of the times, a lifestyle or a business model, it is, first and foremost, an attempt on the part of today's young generation to rethink and reshape the relationship between the city and nature, or society and nature. Once again, the garden is a place of longing, a paradise.

That gardens have always reflected society's relationship with nature and the gardener's relationship with the garden is illustrated by Dagmar Pelger in "Gardening Is Commoning." Using the archetype of the community garden, namely the urban commons, as the basis of her essay, she delves into the history of the development of the garden, with its social, environmental, and political roles: from peasants' kitchen gardens to baronial landscaped gardens to exotic botanical gardens established for exhibition purposes, all to way to modern-day urban community gardens, in which fallow city land is brought back to life.

In early June, I find joy in every green plant in the garden. It slowly becomes obvious which plants will become poppies, mallows, calendula, and tufted violets. I hope that the plants I didn't pull out while weeding are actual chamomile plants. After a few weeks, I discover that real chamomile reseeded itself along the edge of the potato plot, and that I'd cultivated scentless chamomile. In her piece, "A Plea for Weeds," Brunhilde Bross-Burkhardt contemplates the relationship gardeners have with plants they did not intentionally plant. Gardeners can either tolerate weeds (also called *wild plants* and *mulch plants*), include them in their meals, or fight them using conventional methods. In this context, Bross-Burkhardt pleads in favour of tolerating them in the garden. No garden is complete without those plants that simply reappear of their own accord. And is it perhaps not also possible that we might become more open and understanding in our lives outside of gardening if we accept that which does not belong on a smaller scale? The small, often overlooked, or unduly forgotten plants are also examined by Roberta Schneider in her piece,

"In Praise of the Unassuming." Why should moss, so wonderfully soft and verdant, be removed? Is it considered too untidy for the horticulturally minded soul? She clearly illustrates that moss has an aesthetic purpose in other cultures, such as in Japanese gardens. In the Munt la Reita garden, we reach a compromise with respect to weeds: we try to give the plants we have put into the ground enough air to grow by removing the weeds and placing them on top of the mulch as green manure. We try to keep the paths more or less clear and are happy about any plants that self-propagate, such as columbine, lady's mantle, daisies, and St. John's wort.[6]

The amount of work required to weed and prepare a garden of this size means that helping hands are always welcome. Many people help in the garden, and some have been returning to the farm for years and are very familiar with the garden.[7] Everyone plants the seeds of their garden knowledge. In "Among Garden Friends," Miriam Paulsen provides an account of all the things she has learned from her allotment garden neighbours, and how her experience there has broadened her world.

In his text, "Learning by Digging—What You Can Learn from Community Gardening," Severin Halder gives voice to urban gardeners, who talk about what collective activities in the garden can teach at various levels, how you can build knowledge through garden work, and what can be learned from the plants themselves. After all, weeding and removing roots requires knowing how to tell the difference between what needs to be removed and what should stay.

At Munt la Reita, Verena is explaining to a group of young men how to thoroughly remove giant hogweed, which is growing rampant in the garden. Meanwhile, the women are shovelling compost. In her contribution, "Let It Grow," Nicole von Horst explores the question of whether gardening practices are gendered. Do different genders garden differently? Does social gender impact gardening? Everyone gets dirty from garden work; nail beds turn black and everyone sweats. More than physical stamina is required in the garden; mental stamina is also needed. Not everyone is able to withstand long periods of crouching down, rooting through soil, with nothing but their thoughts for company. Most people quickly become bored. We start to see weeds as opponents, categorizing them into different types of challenges, up to the most difficult: to pull out the weed in its entirety, down to the smallest rootlet. "And how do you do that?" My response: "With a great deal of instinct or brute force."

The Munt la Reita garden planting follows the principles of permaculture. Judith Henning, in "Urban Permaculture—City Gardening with a Hidden Agenda," describes what a difference permaculture makes and how it can be implemented in cities, even on a small scale. The fundamental ethical notions behind the natural cultivation of the areas that Henning illustrates in her essay can be applied to both urban and country permaculture projects: mindfully using resources, people, and animals; long-term regeneration cycles, self-limitation, and reallocation; variety rather than monoculture to generate an edible landscape. The differences between permaculture in the city and in the country are considered from the perspective of practical constraints: for example, the question of whether there is fertile, uncontaminated land, which is usually the case in the country, but also the space available to plant and a good supply of compost. According to Henning, these are the prerequisites that city gardeners often need to establish first. Challenges when practising permaculture at mountain elevations include the shorter growing season, low average temperature, and short harvest season. Despite this, a lot more grows at an elevation of 1,400 metres than you might expect.[8]

Planting at Munt la Reita is done following polyculture principles. Swiss chard is interplanted with leeks and red cabbage, with fennel along the edges.[9] We try to optimize the existing area; by interplanting crops, it is more difficult for weeds, diseases, and pests to spread. What is important here, however, is that the plants are companion plants. But we don't take it too seriously. Despite all our efforts, there might be a few lettuce plants beside the celery. According to our guidelines, these two aren't compatible—and, as a matter of fact, when harvest time comes around, it will become apparent that head lettuce didn't stand much of a chance alongside the celery.

As for us, we are fighting our very own battle against the chickens. The garden and the greenhouse are their winter grounds. They spot and peck at the snails, and in the spring we are blessed with almost snail-free lettuce. But when it comes time to move the chickens to their summer fields and to get them to actually stay there, they challenge us in any way they can. The result is high fences and an attempt to sabotage the chicken's takeoff strips from the coop's roof. In the end, we have to retrieve the free-range chickens and cover the exposed ground they've scratched up. The fresh lettuce falls prey to the chickens, not snails.

Summer arrives at the end of June, and it's time to bring in the hay. The garden becomes visibly greener and the plants are growing. The first beds need another weeding. One morning, I'm able to see right through a red currant bush. It wasn't like that the day before. The cabbage moth caterpillars have been ruthlessly eating all the leaves of the red currant bushes. They don't stop until they reach the black currants; they don't like them. We are just as relentless as the caterpillars, and while they continue to eat their way through the shrub, we continue to stoically pick them off the leaves, spraying what is left of the plants with a strong-smelling infusion of wormwood and anise. I learn that stoicism is one of the key virtues of gardening: never give up, and keep on top of it.

It gets warmer and drier. We water more and more. Usually by hand, early in the morning, using water collected in old bathtubs. It now takes four people an hour to do all the watering. Daily, I find myself repeating the guiding principles to occasional and new waterers: "Always water the ground, not the plants. Bee balm likes a strong stream of water straight onto the earth. The potatoes don't need anything." Those parts of the garden that are automatically watered using sprinklers and drip hoses do a lot better: the plants are bigger and grow more quickly. Although the garden is not planted according to what needs more water, in the summer, large portions of the gardens are switched over to automatic watering in the early morning hours. Once again, time plays a significant role. If four people don't have to water, they can do something else. How many people are needed to cultivate a garden this size? Can one efficiently maintain a garden without being a professional vegetable grower? What does *efficiency* mean in an organic garden?

The garden grows and flourishes under the summer sun. The first calendula blossom opens on July 4; we harvest salad greens like misticanza and beautiful trout lettuce, with its delicate red speckles. We savour two bowls of strawberries in July. That's it. This is not the year for strawberries. Poppies in the stone wall, daisies, mallows, and sunflower transform the garden into a colourful pallet. I'm in the middle of the garden, discussing the question of how much garden you need to provide for yourself, a family, an entire team, and still have something to sell at your farm store. When is it not enough, how much is enough, how much is too much?

Visitors to the farm store look at the garden and ask, "What do you do for fertilizer? How do you deal with snails? Aren't they hiding under the mulch?" I tell them about the chickens and how the soil in Ticino, on the southern side of the Alps, is different from the soil on the north side, and that we mulch with a lot of hay. Early in the summer, we fertilized the cabbage plants with compost, but we haven't yet had to water the plants with liquid nettle manure this year.

By the middle of August, it's really hot. In the garden, it's hard to move along the paths because the plants have spread out so much. This is how I vainly tried to imagine the garden in May. We gather the blossoms from calendula, cornflower, tufted violets, bee balm, and mallow for tea, and herbs for the kitchen, and dry them in the drying shed, which is like the garden's treasure vault. Now it's time to harvest currants, despite the fact that the shrubs were stripped bare in June. Almost daily, some good soul is busy preparing a big pot of currants to make jam, jelly, and syrup. We steep chive blossoms in vinegar, and freeze some of the Swiss chard, beans, and zucchini, even if they taste best straight from the garden to the pan. Beets and fennel are consumed more quickly than expected, and the onions are stored in the boiler room to dry. The heads of green and savoy cabbages are as full and beautiful as the moon. We hang them from twine in the cellar and hope they keep. The joy of going into this lush garden and taking what we need is offset by the feeling that it's the garden that is consuming us, and not us consuming the garden. The garden challenges us every day. If we ignore it today, we know there will be twice as much to do tomorrow. There they are again, the joys and struggles of gardening.

I never thought the potatoes I planted in May would develop into anything. In September, it's time to get the harvest out of the ground: crates of large and small tubers. There will be enough for winter. We leave the pointed white cabbage, the kale, the leeks, and the red cabbage in the earth for now. At night, we hear stags roaring in the forest: it is rutting season. Deer love cabbage. In addition to a protective, naturalized hedgerow, a fence bedecked with blinking lights will frighten deer so they don't eat everything in the garden. Snails and chickens seem harmless by comparison.

Speaking of fences: In "A Green Thumb Requires Your Whole Hand," Maximilian Probst takes us on a short trip through the cultural history of the fence, and considers whether the garden fence is actually the beginning of marking private property. Which brings with it a whole host of problems like jealousy and resentment, and is thus, in a figurative sense, the basis for the concepts of property and ownership we still use today. In any case, gardens can be both a blessing and a curse, all while also being utterly ambivalent. An acknowledgement I agree with.

Once again, it's warm enough to sit in the garden. Right in the middle of the garden, among the freshly weeded and mulched paths. This garden doesn't have a spot to relax, with benches or an arbour, like in a landscape or allotment garden, the types of gardens or garden areas that Kristina Vagt takes us to in her essay, "Garden Shows as Driving Force—The Staging of Urban Green Spaces." The main focus in cities and metropolitan areas selected to become sites for horticultural exhibitions, garden shows, and landscaped gardens is relaxation and knowledge transfer, along with outdoor sport, play, and leisure. It's the visitors who take pleasure in being outside and who fill public parks and gardens with life through their activities. By contrast, the garden I'm in is a place that creates work: planting, weeding, watering. But it also rewards us for our work with its vitality, the colours and scents of summer, and a bountiful harvest.

In their relationship with the garden, to circle back to Sarah Thelen, gardeners also express their relationship to the world. Thelen depicts gardeners as attentive administrators who at best interact with the entire world as benevolently and with as much foresight as they might with their own garden. This would be a philosophy of gardening in which gardeners transfer their little observations of the garden to other areas of life and then out into the world. In this way— to paraphrase French landscape architect Gilles Clément— every person who lives responsibly becomes a gardener, and all people become "occupants of a single garden. Whether you live in the city or in the country, the garden is still one and the same: planet Earth."[10] The benevolent gardener, who, on a small scale, does things properly on a larger scale, might not be an achievable ideal. This is precisely why every garden and every gardener is justified. The texts in this book share, from various viewpoints, a wide variety of gardens and thoughts on gardening. But, in the spirit of a *practical philosophy of gardening*, the best thing is to just start: head out into the garden and do something.

When the first snow falls in October, we prune the currant shrubs and tie them together. Winter can come. The chickens have been moved from their summer pasture into the garden. They peck and scratch, and we hope they will gift us with snail-free lettuce next year. The tomatoes didn't turn red; there wasn't enough time or sun. At least green tomatoes can be made into delicious chutney.

Blanka Stolz is one of the founders of the publishing company Mairisch Verlag and spent the better part of two summers in the garden of the Swiss mountain farm Munt la Reita. She would like to thank all the contributors for their commitment and their contributions, Peter Reichenbach for being the driving force behind the project and providing her with the initiative to make the book happen, Daniel Beskos and Hannah Zirkler for their careful reading of the texts, and Elke von Radziewsky for the inspiring phone conversations.

1   Rudolf Borchardt, The Passionate Gardener, trans. Henry Martin, translation copyright © 2006 by Kaspar Borchardt; reproduced courtesy of the publisher, McPherson & Company, on behalf of the translator and copyright owner's estate.

2   The Senn family's organic farm, Munt la Reita, is located in Valle di Campo, a side valley of the Maggia Valley in the canton of Ticino, Switzerland, located about one hour from Locarno by car: www.muntlareita.ch.

3   Maria Thun, The Maria Thun Biodynamic Calendar (Edinburgh: Floris Books, published annually since 1963). Over several years of research conducted in the 1950s, Thun observed a connection between the movement of the moon through the zodiac and the growth of plants depending on when they were planted. Based on this, she divided plants into different types, based on growth. According to the planting calendar, there are days that are best for planting root vegetables (potatoes, celery root, radishes, carrots, etc.), leafy plants (kohlrabi, leeks, parsley, lettuce, spinach, etc.), flower plants (flowers, flowering bulbs, broccoli, etc.), and fruit and seed-producing plants (berries, nuts, fruit, beans, peppers, tomatoes, cucumbers, etc.).

4   Not just sports and fitness magazines proclaim that gardening is a sport and is part of a fitness program; the garden is a place for stretching and doing strength and endurance training. Numerous publications on the topic of yoga for gardening impart a similar message.

5   In more detail: Cordula Kropp, Gärtner(n) ohne Grenzen: Eine neue Politik des "Sowohl-als-auch" urbaner Gärten? [Gardening/Gardeners Without Borders: A New Politics of "both/and" urban gardens?] In Christa Müller (Ed.), Urban Gardening: Über die Rückkehr der Gärten in die Stadt [Urban Gardening: On the Return of Gardens to Cities*] (Munich: Oekom, 2011) 76-87.
    *Translator's note (TN): Unless otherwise noted, all translations of book titles or quoted passages are my own.

6   "Weeds don't disappear" is what we thought when we came up with the name for our publishing house, Mairisch Verlag, in 1999. In the state of Hessen, home to the publishing house and its founders, chickweed is called Mairisch. Legend has it that one of the founders' grandmothers asked if we couldn't do something a bit more useful

than working with books. Like rip out the Mairisch plants. Chickweed is a ground cover that can be found in almost every garden. I removed tonnes of it while at Munt la Reita and enjoyed using it to garnish our lunchtime salads.

7 When I use the word *we*, I am referring to all the people working and helping in the garden. In addition to the family, this includes Philippe, Susanna, Valentina, Mira, Jonas, Kaya, Monika, Coni, Annina, Teuni, and many others.

8 Another well-documented permaculture project that has been implemented for several years at higher elevations is Sepp Holzer's farm, Krameterhof, located in the state of Salzburg: http://www.krameterhof.at/cms60/index.php?id=151.

9 Among others, we use the following companion planting guide: Kurt Forster, Mein Selbstversorger-Garten am Stadtrand: Permakultur auf kleiner Fläche [My Self-Sustaining Garden on the City Outskirts: Small-Space Permaculture] (Staufen i. Br.: ökobuch, 2013). Also recommended: Jutta Langheineken, Christa Weinrich, Schwester Christas Mischkultur: Im Einklang mit der Natur gärtnern [Companion Planting: Gardening in Harmony with Nature] (Fulda: Eugen Ulmer, 2016).

10 Gabriele Detterer, "Die Erde als Garten" [The Planet as a Garden], in Neue Zürcher Zeitung (Zurich, 2011), www.nzz.ch/die-erde-als-garten-1.10402904.

SARAH THELEN

Leaves That Mean the World—How We Express Our Relationship to the World in the Garden

Without a doubt, a garden is artificial. And yet, unlike other products of civilization, a garden exists somewhere between a human construct and a natural environment. A living substance, of its own accord, a garden follows innate and often unpredictable developments—one might say it does what it wants. Plants shoot up, propagate, and grow in unexpected ways. They often don't thrive in the places a gardener provides for them, and instead establish themselves in unplanned spaces. And let's not even start discussing seasonal changes and animal visitors that come and go. A garden continuously moves away from the artifact that it was at the outset, and the gardener has to deal with these changes, one way or the other. And so gardens have a special status among man-made things: they show the relationship a person has with their environment. This isn't just about the gardener's direct dealings with the natural things making up a garden, their approach to weather and climate, and exchanges with those who see or use the garden. It is also about their relationship to the environment in a much broader sense: their connection to the rest of the world.

Let's first look at the relationship the gardener has with their immediate surroundings. We can assume a garden was planned in a certain way and that it should be preserved in the same way. This applies to a formal, modern designer garden, but also to a cottage garden—that is, the traditional English perennial garden—in which certain flower compositions and plant arrangements are provided.[1] Let's also assume that the plants selected for this design aren't ideal for the soil, the climatic conditions, or the adjacent plants (which also occurs—often, plants in designer gardens are chosen primarily for their aesthetic features, even if their requirements don't match the location).

Should a garden to which these two cases apply remain the way it is, it would have to be meticulously maintained, or the design would be out the window. Strictly speaking, change doesn't stop, because even the act of constantly taking measures to counteract natural development, such as pruning shrubs, cutting back vigorous growth, and replanting whatever has died off, implies change to the garden. Take, for example, the gardeners whose relationship to their immediate environment is characterized by attempts to impose their will on the natural climate, soil, and plant characteristics through constant, energy-sapping work. The desire to conquer the environment manifests itself as much through garden work as it does through an awareness of the environment and responding to it in a beneficial way. Here it becomes apparent that the garden, even in a more general sense, is also a "reflection of the connection between people and their environment," as landscape architect George B. Tobey puts it.[2] The ways in which people exercise their transformative influence, and how and to what extent they control, support, hinder, or leave (or attempt to leave) unhindered the elements in their environment in order to achieve a synergistic effect, is represented by their approach to gardening—and is more or less representative of their approach to other areas of life.

This desire to uncompromisingly impose one's will, against all odds, almost never leads to success. Most people learn this at a young age. And of course this also applies to gardens;

living matter abides by its own rules. However, the fact that an intelligent response to the surrounding circumstances has to be more sensible, more efficient, and more favourable is just one reason to strive for a positive and co-operative relationship with the garden and, beyond that, with the entire world. The second reason is that this corresponds to our human nature. If our care results in a magnificent, healthy garden, we're happy. If we are in sync with our surroundings, we're more content and happy than when we're not. Here, philosophy provides us with a few explanations.

For this, we have to start with the question of the meaning of life, which leads us to questions of what it means to be good and benevolent. Every single person (who is not acutely struggling with daily survival) desires to give their existence meaning. This thought is particularly prevalent among existential philosophers and their pioneers: Nietzsche says that individuals create a world of notions and symbols to give themselves meaning;[3] Heidegger states that the fear of a pointless life can only be overcome by creating situations that provide the meaning that is missing (being as projection);[4] and Sartre speaks of the inevitable freedom of meaningful self-creativity—that is, of a quest for meaning that we cannot get around.[5] Individual meaning is often perceived as existing not just in purely self-centred petty fears and envies, but rather, as devoting one's life to the well-being of something that is outside one's self. Whether this desire originates from the social disposition of human nature and its connected altruism or is established merely on the basis of a need to be acknowledged is another matter. In this context, Rousseau, for example, speaks of natural human compassion.[6] Professor of ethics Peter Singer cites psychological studies according to which people who have the well-being of others in mind are generally more content than those who only put their own interests first.[7]

Philosopher Iris Murdoch states that goodness goes hand in hand with the attempt to see the non-self—that is, to turn toward others.[8] This fulfilling benevolence doesn't need to have other people as its object; it can also focus on other areas, as exhibited by the widespread sympathy for organizations devoted to the protection of animals and nature. Even an emotional commitment to the preservation of historic monuments can contain a benevolence that is released from the self and thereby generates a sense of purpose. If we take a look at the range of publications on the topic of meaningful life, we discover the following: if we pay someone else to undertake altruistic actions on our behalf (for example, in the form of an annual monetary contribution toward an aid organization), this seems to make us much less satisfied than if we actually undertake a benevolent act ourselves—if possible, within our own living environment. The term *benevolence* is of particular use here, because it does not imply sacrificial behaviour or concrete action to support those in need. Benevolence, rather, refers to the harmonious relationship with the environment, goodwill toward everyone and everything you come into contact with. Naturally, as a result of this type of goodwill toward everyone, conflicts emerge between the idea of the good for one and the good for another.

Earlier, we deal with people's altruistic tendencies; now, we find ourselves moving into the field of ethics. Conflicts of interest can be avoided by borrowing from Kant's moral philosophy: one of his formulations on the categorical imperative states that we should never act such that we treat humanity as a means only, but always as an end unto itself.[9] If we shift our gaze from humanity to include everything living, what this means in the context of a garden is that a purely purpose-driven approach should never be the sole basis for decision-making. Instead, animals and plants, even if they do not serve an immediate purpose, should be seen as ends unto themselves. All decisions pertaining to the well-being of one versus the well-being of another should therefore be made under the premise (generally speaking) of doing as little harm as possible—regardless of whether this decision has a direct benefit or not.

Once you've established a good relationship with your garden, you have a decent chance of developing an equally benevolent and cleverly co-operative relationship with the rest of the world. Or perhaps this relationship is already in place and becomes especially apparent in the garden. The French landscape architect Gilles Clément even describes the planet on the whole as a garden, when referring to the 1990s exhibition in Paris, *Le Jardin Planétaire*:

> [...] the earth regarded as an environment set aside for life is a closed space [...] As soon as this observation has been made, it reminds all human beings, whose earthly existence is so fleeting, of their responsibilities... so they have become gardeners.[10]

Such benevolence toward the world could manifest itself in the garden as room for all potential users of the garden—play areas for children, places to sit or lie down for those seeking rest and relaxation, and stimulating green areas or thoughtful paths for walkers, depending on the type of garden and who might be using it.

But benevolence doesn't stop there. It extends to all parties: not just people, but also plants and wild animals would be considered so-called users of the garden. They'd be given—in keeping with Kant's categorical imperative— enough free space to coexist without causing mutual suffering. The garden becomes a balanced space, a peaceful space, in which the fight for survival—that is, the struggle for personal gain—is switched off as much as possible. Good planning when creating a garden also helps prevent the emergence of struggles from the outset. A smart and prudent gardener selects not just the plants, but also the planting locations, and the relationship of garden areas to one another, so that everything planted can thrive, unimpeded by climate, soil, and light conditions, inappropriate neighbouring plants, etc., that might inhibit development and cause the plants to become unhealthy.

This forward-thinking activity for the plants' well-being also impacts the gardener's well-being. Plants that are not compromised are more resistant to pests and illnesses, need less care, better fulfil their purpose (whether decorative, fruit-bearing, providing shade, etc.), and do not have to be replaced as often. It goes without saying that the owner of a private garden first has to find out what thrives in their soil and what does not, through trial and error and by querying the neighbours. What is implied here is the knowledge gardeners have about what works and what does not: "Willows belong near creeks, and spruce trees belong in the forest; anyone wishing to do otherwise will regret it," says gardening author Eva Demski with respect to the relationship between insightful planning and the well-being of plants and gardeners.[11]

Nowadays, many garden architects and designers try to take into consideration the climatic, soil, and light requirements of plants. For example, Henk Gerritsen studied plant communities in temperate climates in their natural habitats to be able to recreate them in his Priona Tuinen gardens in the Netherlands.[12] His horticultural commandment: "You shouldn't complain." Your horticultural pride should be set aside in favour of the natural properties of plants and animals.

In order to maintain a state of equilibrium in a garden, the gardener must intervene, and stop or remove elements that disrupt the balance. This applies to, among others, invasive weeds, which, because of their vigorous growth and ability to easily reproduce, quickly drown out other cultivated or wild plants. Or pests, which, by infesting fruit, flowers, or leaves, endanger the existence of a certain type of plant in the garden. Crucial in a balanced approach is to recognize that not all freely growing wild plants or wild shoots of cultivated plants need to be eradicated, just as all insects, snails, etc., that are not explicitly useful should not be seen as pests needing to be destroyed. Disruptive and destructive elements are not tolerated, but everything else would be welcome and supported as best as possible, as long as the other living components of the garden are not endangered. If, for example, a gardener discovered bats, they could attempt to protect them by providing a bat house or some other type of shelter. Butterflies and moths could be provided with a wildflower meadow or an insect hotel. If seeds from the neighbour's columbine were to end up in another garden (they like to propagate), the gardener in question would find pleasure in allowing them to grow in areas where they are not disruptive, even if they had not intentionally been planted there.

If you look at a garden this way, the gardener only needs to intervene to keep things in check, with the exception of measures they themselves have determined necessary; the existing living structure does not always have to impose upon the system-imminent predisposition in other outcomes. A problematic relationship, in which the gardener needs to constantly exert considerable effort to control the plants' natural tendencies, runs contrary to the desire of well-being for everyone. The goal is to avoid a conflict-prone gardening situation. This can be done with forward-thinking planning, as described above, which can, for example, prevent the planting of a large tree in a garden that is too small for it, resulting in the need to forcibly keep the tree small.

The gardener's attitude is also essential. Seeing the garden as a living fabric sets the groundwork for a relationship in which all parties benefit—but particularly the gardener, as the gardener is spared a lot of work, and the garden becomes a positive experience. I am personally acquainted with garden owners who want exposed earth around the plants in their gardens and who constantly have to work at maintaining this state, which runs counter to nature. Others, exhibiting unilateral thinking, set traps for squirrels because they're worried about nesting birds and their fledglings (even though squirrels very rarely eat them); others kill frogs and toads they happen upon in their gardens, because they find these animals disgusting or don't want to have to listen to them all night long. Gardening that suppresses normal life processes, and that emphasizes the garden as a polished lifestyle product that is absolutely shaped, leaves no room for more profound experiences of joy and satisfaction, and is conceivably a far cry from generally beneficent gardening.

Someone with a healthy, benevolent attitude toward their environment, and the rest of the world, would also let this benevolence prevail in the garden, thereby creating a garden in an almost automatic state of equilibrium. The relationship could also have the opposite effect: It's unlikely that anyone who has undertaken the reasonable planning of a garden could avoid applying knowledge acquired through that process to other areas of life. Remember Clément, who sees a gardener in every person who lives responsibly.

In summary, and for all types of gardens, one could say: the best possible garden is one that expresses a relationship with the world born of the best intentions; includes plants, animals, and people in and around the garden; and last but not least, includes the gardener themselves. If one were to express the nature of the best possible gardener as a metaphor, they would be a prudent administrator who establishes enduring peace in their garden. They would create infrastructure (plants, paths, ponds, etc.) from which everyone would benefit, and would make every effort to help those beings living within their sphere of influence. Where there are inevitable conflicts of interest, the gardener would resolve them with as little harm as possible to the participants, and overall. It would be desirable if gardeners—and everyone, really—could develop this kind of relationship with their environment, and bring benevolence and intelligent forward planning to their worldly interactions, all while taking responsibility for their personal gain and well-being. A "philosophy of gardening," in reference to this book's title, could also be seen as a philosophy that takes shape within the limited area of the garden, but should also apply to the world as a whole.

In her thesis, **Dr. Sarah Thelen** wrote about the garden's cultural role. Her own garden is located on a dry, limestone ridge in the heart of the city of Kassel, which is why she knows how difficult but rewarding gardening can be.

1 Hanno Rauterberg. "Das Glück ist grün" [Happiness Is Green], in Die Zeit (Hamburg, May 24, 2012), 44.

2 George B. Tobey, A History of Landscape Architecture: The Relationship of People to Environment (New York et al: Elsevier Publishing Company, 1973), ix.

3 Friedrich W. Nietzsche, The Gay Science, trans. Thomas Common (New York: The Macmillan Company, 1924).

4 Martin Heidegger, Contributions to Philosophy (From Enowning) (Studies in Continental Thought), trans. Parvis Emad and Kenneth Maly [1936–1938], Volume 65 of the collection. (Bloomington: Indiana University Press, 2000).

5 Jean-Paul Sartre, Being and Nothingness: An Essay in Phenomenological Ontology, [1943] trans. Sarah Richmond. (Abingdon: Routledge, 2018).

6 Jean-Jacques Rousseau, Émil, or On Education, [1762], original title: Émile ou de l'éducation, trans. Barbara Foxley, published as a part of the Everyman's Library collection (London: J. M. Dent and Sons Ltd and New York: E. P. Dutton and Co., 1911).

7   Peter Singer, "Is Luxury Immoral?" interview by Stefan Klein in We Are
    All Stardust: Scientists Who Shaped Our World Talk about Their Work,
    Their Lives and What They Still Want to Know (New York: The Experi-
    ment, 2015), 110.

8   See Iris Murdoch, The Sovereignty of Good (Oxford: Routledge, [1970]
    2001).

9   Immanuel Kant, Collected Works, Royal Prussian Academy of Sciences
    (Ed.) Vol. 1–22, Deutsche Akademie der Wissenschaften zu Berlin (Ed.)
    Vol. 23, Akademie der Wissenschaften zu Göttingen (Ed.) from Vol. 24.
    Reprints of 1962 edition et seq. (Berlin, New York: De Gruyter) IV 462.
    (The information is related to the volume and the page.)

10 Gilles Clément in: Virgilio and Matteo Vercelloni, Inventing the Garden,
    (Los Angeles: J. Paul Getty Museum, 2010), 10.

11 Eva Demski, "Der Garten meiner Mutter" [My Mother's Garden], in
    Deutsche Gesellschaft für Gartenkunst und Landschaftskultur (Ed.),
    Private Gartenkultur. Geschichte, Moden und Trends, (Munich:
    Callwey, 2011), 9.

12 Leo den Dulk, "Schachspiel, Schauspiel, Gartenkunst" [Chess Game,
    Performance, Garden Art], in Gartenkultur (Berlin: DGGL Hessen
    Newsletter, 2011), 18.

Among Garden Friends

"It's all the rage again, gardening and that kind of stuff. You're totally on trend."

"Mm."

"Can you actually spend the night there, too?"

"Well, in theory, but it's not really allowed, and I live just around the corner."

"Are there lots of strict rules, too?"

"There are rules, but they're actually not that strict."

Urban and guerrilla gardening, seed bombs, Farmville, organic produce boxes—it seems that anything to do with gardening, vegetables, and greenery is back in style, at least if you go by the raised beds featured in the weekend news, the local papers' horticultural meanderings, and the flourishing blog biotopes. In response to the classic rhetorical small-talk question "Did you know that the German bimonthly gardening, home, and women's magazine *Landlust* sells more copies than the German weekly news magazine *Der Spiegel*? And almost twice as many as the German national weekly newspaper *Die Zeit?*"[1] one might counter: "No way. And did you know that the 278 small allotment gardens in Leipzig with more than 39,000 plots covering a surface area of approximately 1,240 hectares form a significant portion of the green lung, namely 30 percent?"[2] So much for the statistics.

Now What?

In the Allotment Garden Capital, as Leipzig, Germany, is unofficially called, one of these 278 gardens—which, with names like Sommerwind (Summer Wind), Hoffnung (Hope), Nach Feierabend (After Work), and Froschburg (Frog Castle), are so enticing they literally get green thumbs twitching—is called Kolonie Dr. Schreber (Dr. Schreber's Colony). Here, the new hype over garden plots is still not very apparent. Of course, young garden worshippers are welcomed into the fold, but the community of gardening friends is, on average, an older sort. There are quite a few garden gnomes, solar lights lining the pathways, colourful plastic Easter eggs adorning shrubs at Easter, rain barrels, compost piles, lots of bare skin, flagpoles, delimiting boxwood hedges, controlled wild growth, foxes, and raccoons. And a few rules. While not necessarily an expression of oft-quoted petit-bourgeois conformism, they do serve to preserve the charitable status of the allotment garden association.

Incidentally, the person after whom the garden is named, Daniel Gottlob Moritz Schreber, didn't care about any of this in the least. In addition to his rather questionable views regarding raising children and young people, he also promoted the benefits of outdoor activities. This in turn inspired Leipzig school director Ernst Innozenz Hauschild to form an association of organized outdoor areas where families could play, and thus the first Schreberverein, or allotment garden association, was named in Schreber's honour in 1864. At the time, however, the association's namesake was already six feet under. And so ends that story.

"Have you always been so into gardening?"

"Not really."

"But did you have a garden growing up?"

"My grandma had one. We only had a balcony."

When talking about the benefits of this idyllic life, you inevitably stumble down the path of clichés: your very own spot in the country, working with your hands, digging around in the earth and being one with Mother Nature, relaxation, fresh air, exercise ("No need to go to the gym anymore. It's good for your back."). Discovering skills you thought you'd lost or, even better, never had (such as cutting back shrubs at random so they bloom next year). You get something in return: you see the results of your work, you can harvest your own fruit and vegetables ("Google 'what can you do with Swiss chard?'"). Never mind the floral splendour of tulips and narcissus, magnolias, peonies, lilacs, lavender, Lady's mantle ("Look at how the water droplets collect in its leaves!"), dahlias ("Dig them out over the winter, store them in a dark, dry place, and then plant them again early summer, easy peasy..."), and asters—to name just a few, more or less in their order of seasonal appearance.

Things you didn't know you'd have to deal with:
1. The ticking of the floral clock

"And the neighbours? How are they?"

"Oh, they're okay."

"You've been lucky."

"Mm."

The first visit to the allotment garden, a neighbour introduces himself: "Hi, I'm your garden friend, Jürgen." He explains the difference between a shovel and a spade to the ambitious hobbyist, brutally unearthing the first toad from its winter hibernation. Folding chairs, bedecked with floral patterns from the seventies, are cast off by the well-established members of the garden colony and happily make their way over the fence to the newly initiated, who also learn how to process the stray peaches from Jürgen's tree that fall onto their side of the fence. On holidays, in accordance with the occasion, glasses clink: shots of schnapps on Men's Day (the German equivalent of Father's Day), piccolos on Mother's Day, and while his wife is pruning roses, setting tulips, and planting dahlias, Jürgen pushes his wheelbarrow, loaded with bags of potting soil and manure, works the soil, repairs fences, and relaxes in his garden swing, from where he feeds local song-birds and squirrels by tossing them nuts and bread.

Things you didn't know you'd have to deal with:
2. Division of labour behind the garden fence

"Why do you even have a garden?"

"It was a gift. From friends. They paid for the transfer fee and a year's rent."

"What do you mean? So it doesn't belong to you?"

"No, we're renting it, so to speak."

"Is it expensive?"

"Nope, about two hundred euros per year."

A nice gift, at least from a romantic viewpoint. On closer inspection, the nearly two hundred square metres turn out to be a rundown heap of leaves and a garden full of blackberry brambles and overgrown paving bricks. The patio is decked out in moth-eaten AstroTurf, and as for the inside of the little house, you can admire the often-invoked talent for improvisation born during the communist era. Everyone is overjoyed—hooray, a project! Challenge accepted. The voluntary spring cleanup day finds us enthusiastically weeding and digging. Everyone is enjoying themselves.

After several small pickup truck loads of garbage are delivered to the dump, it's time to start planning the infrastructure. Paths? Isn't a dirt track enough? What about concrete slabs? A pebble pathway is much nicer. Other garden friends warn us: the weeds will take over in no time. We assure them we'll manage the few weeds. As for painting the arbour: environmentally friendly paint or oil-based, so it lasts forever? What about vegetables? Definitely! But flowers, too. And the toilet: a portable chemical toilet or compostable bark mulch in a certified plastic bag? First, let's plant an apple tree.

Things you didn't know you'd have to deal with:
3. Your friends' poop

"So what did you get?"

"Two apple trees, a sour cherry tree, a plum tree, currant and gooseberry shrubs, raspberries, wild strawberries—those little ones—herbs, flowers, and whatever else people grow."

"And what are those?"

"Potatoes, lettuce, cucumbers, radishes, carrots, beans, or even tomatoes."

"Isn't it cheaper to buy your tomatoes in the grocery store? If you think of all the watering and stuff."

"Not really."

The relationship to fruits and vegetables changes over time. A completely new appreciation develops, because a tomato—one that comes from a plant you've lovingly nurtured since planting a seed in a coir-peat wafer on your windowsill, then repotted, planted in the garden, staked, pruned, and watered—tastes better than any other tomato, as long as it hasn't fallen victim to the dreaded tomato blight. There's no way in hell you'd let it go bad in some forgotten corner of your fridge. You learn a multitude of ways to prepare the millions of zucchini. The fruits of the earth now determine daily life: I guess we can't go to the lake, the cherries won't pick themselves. What will we do with them? They won't keep forever. Let's can them. But of course they need to be pitted first. Do I even have enough jars? They can be weighed using the scales in the supermarket... And before you know it, night turns into day, and a delicious sour cherry compote is ready to enjoy.

Things you didn't know you'd have to deal with:
4. Pickling versus making preserves

"Do you have parties sometimes?"

"Well, every now and then we have a barbecue."

"Oh, cool. Do the neighbours join you?"

"Not often."

On the local colony's website, under Garden Laws, is the following statement: "Under normal conditions, relations over the garden fence should be peaceful. In case of disagreements, organizing a collective afternoon barbecue might help."[3] There are no differences of opinion, so friends come by for a barbecue and to assess the progress. They praise the ingenious bedding system, tilled following the guidelines of

crop rotation; delight in the plant structures; leaf through
John Seymour's self-sufficiency bible;[4] play Yahtzee under the
overgrown pergola; poke fun at the mail-order copper-wire
slug barrier, meant to protect the defenceless lettuce from
insatiably greedy snail mouths; let mosquitoes bite them;
help turn the compost and mow the lawn; or just hang out,
nibbling on berries, beer, and sausages.

A raccoon comes by and lurks on the greenhouse roof, lying
in wait for leftovers from the barbecue. It's really, really nice.

Things you didn't know you'd have to deal with:
5. Nighttime raccoon photography

"But aren't there mostly older people? Or are lots of them
younger now?"

"There are younger people, but older ones, too."

The garden kitty-corner to us is owned by two sisters, Käthe
and Edith. They've been keeping their garden for more than
forty years. They're not philistines in the least. Their garden
is resplendent with flowers, and includes a small pond and
a winding path, at the end of which the two gazebo gals can
often be seen sunbathing in their bikinis. When it comes to
identifying plants, Ms. Käthe really knows her stuff, and she
usually even knows the Latin names. When we want to know
whether or not something is a weed, she advises us to wait and
see instead of pulling it out. And she always has something
to share: raspberry canes, ground cover, or a plump chicken.
Their pergola is overgrown with a Ukrainian grapevine,
also obtained from a garden friend; the lush grapes on the
imported vine would change even Aesop's fox's mind about
snubbing sour grapes.

Things you didn't know you'd have to deal with:
6. The common name for Allium aflatunense is
Persian onion

Living with a garden plot offers natural answers to the really big questions. Flora and fauna follow simple rules: old things disappear, new things appear; some things graze (snails), other things are razed (lettuce); good stuff gets thrown into the mix (only healthy plant remnants are added to the compost, except for weeds, which have to be chopped up first), bad stuff gets nixed (so to the recycling yard).

The weekly lawn mowing is ideal for musing on the eternal return. And the question of whether anything makes sense at all is answered as you harvest the first fruits of your labour—in the form of strawberries, tomatoes, or potatoes—with a loud "Yes!"—or when you have pulled weeds from the community path for the hundredth time, muttering a slightly annoyed, "I guess so." In the school of gardening, sometimes you have to serve detention, but it's always worth it.

"It really is a lot of work, this gardening thing."

"Mm."

"But it can be nice."

"Mm."

"Are there any openings in your community gardens?"

"You'll have to check. Don't think so, not right now."

The peach tree in the neighbour's garden was felled. It was already quite big and old, and maybe even a bit diseased. Garden friend Jürgen has been visiting less and less often. His vision isn't that good anymore, which is why he always comes slowly up to the fence, so he can recognize his neighbours. His wife prunes roses, sets tulips, and plants dahlias. She pushes wheelbarrows loaded with bags of potting soil and manure, works the soil, and apologizes that the fence has not yet been repaired. Garden friend Jürgen relaxes in his swing, where he listens to the local songbirds' free concert.

Things you know you absolutely still want to do: 1. Spend the night in the garden; 2. Have a barbecue with the neighbours; 3. Plant a peach tree; 4. Photograph a fox; 5. Build an outdoor shower; 6. Wait for something to move into the birdhouse; 7. Repair the eavestroughs; 8. And the garden fence; 9. Boil more jam; 10. Eat.

Miriam Paulsen lives in Leipzig, where, for the past ten years, she has been running a concept store called Tschau Tschüssi featuring young designers and stationery. Before this, she studied sociology and German. In addition to the day-to-day of running the store, she organizes exhibits, markets, and workshops, and works as a freelance author and editor. She gardens in Dr. Schreber's Colony.

1   Source: statista.com.

2   Source: City of Leipzig.

3   http://www.schreber-leipzig.de/vereinsleben/rechtliches

4   John Seymour, The Self-sufficient Gardener: A Complete Guide to Growing and Preserving All Your Own Food (London: Dorling Kindersley, 1978).

BRUNHILDE BROSS-BURKHARDT

A Plea for Weeds

In every garden there grows vegetation that wasn't intentionally planted by the gardener: namely, weeds. Weeds like nettles, speedwell, and Creeping Charlie, which seem to appear
of their own accord. So, is this a plea for weeds? Not quite.

Communion with Weeds

Having studied vegetation science, I generally like all plants,
even those labelled *weeds*. As a gardener myself, however, I'm
ambivalent about them. Weeds, for me, I must admit, are
both a passion and a burden. Recently, though, the pendu-
lum has been swinging more toward the latter. Objectively,
dealing with the excessive growth of weeds in my vegetable
and perennial beds and pathways has taken up quite a bit
of the rather limited time I have to spend in the garden as
a gardening author. I quarrel with myself over the fact that
I have to spend time doing such useless work and that there
is nobody within kilometres to do it for me. I can't help but
think of Sisyphus. A few decades ago I didn't have to worry;
at first, my garden was pretty much free of weeds. At some
point in those early days, a rather severe hailstorm shredded
anything green. Afterward, I was happy about every plant
that spontaneously sprouted from the bare earth, covering it
in a semblance of greenery.

The weed-free state was short-lived. A rich variety of vegetation quickly grew, because I wasn't overly fastidious and

left a few plants that bloomed and fructified, scattering their seeds and multiplying. I find the individual shapes of wild plants just as aesthetically pleasing as ornamental plants. I like when the nettle-leaved bellflower unexpectedly makes an appearance in a perennial bed or when bindweed takes over a chain-link fence. Things like this can't be planned; they develop naturally.

I also feel that my slightly weedy garden also reflects who I am as a person: I welcome anything new and unplanned, and have no taste for anything strictly regulated or angular. I like to let nature take its course. This gives me the opportunity to see how the vegetation will develop. And this is where my professional interest kicks in.

Weeds Are Evidence of Vitality in Habitats

Wherever I find myself, whether at home or elsewhere, I make note of the plant species growing in a given location, which tells me a lot about the soil and microclimate. Weeds are referred to as *indicator plants* in technical jargon because they are pretty accurate in indicating the properties of a specific environment. For example, common horsetail is always an indicator of standing water, a high water table, and stagnant water in the substrate. I find wastelands and embankments particularly interesting. I never find it boring to travel by train or to wait at train stations, because railway gravel is always home to special flora. This act of observing has been a habit of mine since my student days. Vegetation composition fascinates me, both from the aspect of spatial coexistence and temporal succession.

So I find it extremely interesting to observe the development of the vegetation in my garden over decades. Some plant species appear; others recede. Years ago, the night-flowering catchfly—an intoxicatingly scented night-blooming flower—suddenly appeared in my vegetable beds. Plants that like warmer temperatures, such as cockspur grass or manyseed goosefoot, have also found their way here and spread through my garden beds. Pretty and long-flowering red hemp-nettle popped up overnight in my planters and pots. Usually, I spot them growing on railway embankments. The reddish leaves and egg yolk–yellow flowers of the creeping wood sorrel have long claimed spots in my pots and strawberry beds and show no signs of leaving. It's often unclear how all these newcomers ended up in the garden: whether they got there on their own (airborne, via animals that transported them, via unclean seeds, or in potting soil) or whether I was the one who helped them move into my garden. Because I quite often find myself on botanical forays, I sometimes unintentionally transport fruit and seeds to my garden—whether they are attached to my shoes or clothes, or via a wildflower bouquet. Other times, when I'm out exploring vegetation, I bring back fruit or seeds (for example, wild carrot seeds) and scatter them in the garden, in the hopes they'll germinate and establish themselves in their new environment.

Some cultivars have also gone to seed and are looking for a spot to put down roots. I like to call these species "garden vagabonds." In particular, I'm referring to sweet cicely, with its fernlike leaves; rose campion, with its velvety, bluish-green leaves; or the sweetly scented yellow corydalis.

In my garden, they are allowed to stay. I feel a very close, even emotional, bond with all plants. But I, too, exclude some plants. Plants with a huge network of roots, like common horsetail, ground elder, and field bindweed, which require a lot of weeding, are not plants I want in my garden. I also remove blackberry brambles and woody seedlings. Otherwise, my garden would turn into brush, and in no time, a forest of sorts. And then it would be close to impossible to plant any crops.

Organic farmers and gardeners also have to fight weeds with all the methods available to them, from tilling to hoeing to flame-weeding. Otherwise, the competitive weeds would crowd out or suppress the weaker crop-bearing plants, and in the end, there would be nothing to harvest.

My guiding principle as an individual gardener is to practise tolerance.

Fighting a Losing Battle

Compared to my residential surroundings, however, my tolerant approach to weeds is like fighting a losing battle. All I have to do is look at the gardens in my neighbourhood. Not a weed to be seen. The neighbours, whom I secretly call "anal-retentive gardeners,"[1] fervently pull, rip, and dig every weed out of crevices, or hoe them out of gardens. "Weeds" have to be gotten rid of; they have to be kept under control. Only those plants that were purchased at a garden store are allowed to exist in their gardens. A garden should be as tidy as a living room. Or as scrupulously cleaned and tidily trimmed as a German cemetery. And this objective is pursued using all the equipment on display in the garden centre, and often with much physical energy. They are as likely to pull out harmless nettle as wild clematis or ivy.

The common gardener believes a weed is any plant that disturbs them, that goes against their sense of order or obsessive cleanliness. At least these anal-retentive gardeners don't use herbicides, but rather, mechanically spend their days on a cushion or knee protectors, working their way through the weeds. I can understand why, when kneeling gets to be too much, they are quick to replace their gardens with gravel or pave them over, to finally be done with the tedious work of eradicating weeds.

Weeds Awaken Potentially Primal Fears

I know I can't change the attitudes of anal-retentive gardeners. They don't want to hear explanations or information about the important environmental roles played by weeds—not even about the direct benefits as pollinator meadow plants. I can only shake my head and try to imagine how these people perceive the flora—especially the wild flora—growing around them. When they're working in the garden, they inevitably come face-to-face with it. But they probably only see an undefined mass and don't notice the subtle variations. Sometimes I hear them use ugly terms when talking about plants; *dirt* is harmless by comparison. Anal-retentive gardeners have absolutely no desire to learn what the species are called, let alone how they propagate and spread, or which insects and butterflies they provide habitats for. I imagine that out-of-control vegetation arouses their primal fears. Primal fears of being devoured alive by the wilderness... Now, that's an opportunity for a good psychological study.

By the way, my thoughts on how people see plants put me in good company: in his novel *Steppenwolf*, Hermann Hesse also dealt with the topic of how gardeners perceive plants...

> Imagine a garden with a hundred kinds of trees, a thousand kinds of flowers, a hundred kinds of fruit and vegetables. Suppose, then, that the gardener of this garden knew no other distinction than between edible and inedible; nine-tenths of this garden would be useless to him. He would pull up the most enchanting flowers and hew down the noblest trees and even regard them with a loathing and envious eye.[2]

Language Reveals a Lot

Gardeners and weeds—they could provide psychologists and sociologists with so much research material. An obvious approach is on the linguistic level. The German word for weed is *Unkraut*. As in English, the prefix *un* in German gives the word an opposite or negative connotation, thereby transforming the German word *Kraut*, meaning herb, into something unwanted. In English, also, the word *weed* implies something negative. Take, for example, the proverb "Ill weeds grow apace," which infers that worthless people will always flourish, just as worthless weeds will always thrive, while the plants we value will only grow in our gardens with endless care and attention. Weeds are generally referred to in their plural form. A weed is rarely on its own—it usually appears with several others, and/or a variety of other weeds. The *Canadian Oxford Dictionary* defines a weed as "a wild plant growing where it is not wanted, especially among crops or garden plants." However, this definition in relation to farming and gardening falls short. Plants commonly defined as weeds grow not only in farm fields and gardens, but also in the wild along trails, in the gaps between cobblestones and pavement, in lawns, or under hedges.

Let Creeping Charlie Be

Common parlance expresses so much. From the fact that, for some time now, many have been circumventing the term *weeds*, referring to them instead as *wild plants* or *natural flora*, one can conclude that there's a shift afoot, and that a certain tolerance is taking hold.

Without consistent weed control, professional farms— whether conventional or organic, the only difference is the methods used—would be unsuccessful. After all, humankind needs to be fed. However, the weeding done in a private garden is often excessive or even unnecessary, especially in all the gardens without crop-bearing plants. Allowing Creeping Charlie or Creeping Jenny to grow under shrubs would be a start. Weeds as a showpiece in the garden, as a consciously incorporated counterpoint to the all-pervasive stone-covered, barren front yard—that would be something! So, this is a plea on behalf of nettles, speedwell, and company, with their intriguing shapes and multitude of ecological roles: let them embellish cultivated gardens and settlement areas. I am committed to it!

The agricultural scientist and specialist journalist **Dr. Brunhilde Bross-Burkhardt**, located in Langenburg (Baden-Württemberg), is committed to botany and organic farming and gardening. Her goal is to raise awareness of and maybe even encourage fascination for natural interconnections through her books and magazine articles, as well as through excursions in the great outdoors. www.bross-burkhardt.de

1   TN: The German text uses the term *Kehrwoche* to describe the "anal-retentive" gardener. This term is common to an area of southern Germany called Swabia, where people living in multi-unit homes share the responsibility of keeping shared spaces (usually the stairwell, the landings, the foyer, and sometimes even the sidewalk) clean. Each person is assigned a "week of sweeping" ("Kehr," derived from the verb *kehren*, means sweep; "Woche," means week) and must adhere to that schedule, as cleanliness is a point of pride in this region, and messiness is frowned upon.

2   Hermann Hesse, Steppenwolf, trans. Basil Creighton, rev. Walter Sorrell (London: Penguin Books, 1965), 79.

ROBERTA SCHNEIDER

In Praise of the Unassuming

"Now, a Japanese garden is not a flower garden; neither is it made for the purpose of cultivating plants. In nine cases out of ten, there is nothing in it resembling a flower bed."[1] Although these words were written by Lafcadio Hearn over one hundred years ago, they still ring true. That's why, even now, nine out of ten Japanese gardens are a source of pleasure for people who want nothing to do with flower beds.

It was in gardens like these that, during my last stay in the Land of the Rising Sun, I fell in love with several plants. Mind you, they were winter-hardy plants, which is why I was determined to grow them in my garden—which admittedly only consists of three 30 x 100 centimetre wooden boxes. Still, what a relief to not have to keep everything in pots that then have to be squeezed onto overly full windowsills during the colder months, creating the perfect environment for an overabundance of spider mites!

But first of all, I had to find the plants in question—easier said than done in Germany. There is something about them that gives them no staying power on the German market. I have since found out why: in those dubious identification books that sort plants by the colour of their blooms, they're listed under the categories *green flowers* or *indistinguishable.* Or not at all—because, as flowerless plants, they often don't even make it into these guides, which normally concentrate on flowering plants.

Houttuynia cordata

Buying a *Houttuynia cordata,* the leaves of which can be used to make a very healthy tea, proved to be a challenge because of its various chemotypes. Chemotypes are variants within a plant subspecies that differ in chemical composition. Since these compounds are only relevant to people with specialized interests, the chemotype isn't usually listed for plants that are available for purchase. This means there's little hope of finding out whether it's the citrus-flavoured Japanese chemotype or the Chinese chemotype with a scent reminiscent of coriander before purchasing the plant. In the end, the chemotype becomes irrelevant when you notice that most of the *Houttuynia* on the market are variegated. This transforms an unassuming but majestic plant with green, heart-shaped leaves and white false flowers, which look a bit similar to Japanese dogwood but are less elegant, into an unpleasantly piebald plant that, as soon as it appears in the spring, looks like it's about to lose them, bringing the frightening reminder that fall is approaching. When you see that, it no longer matters which chemotype you get—as long as the plant isn't variegated.

It's no coincidence that variegated sounds like adulterated. Because the poor plant isn't piebald by accident: it's fully intentional. "It's a foliage plant," say those who like it, or those wanting to talk others into purchasing one. "It will brighten the dark corners of your garden," they argue. Nobody asks the plant if it would rather stand in a lighter corner of the garden, because it's not needed there. If you have a dark corner in your garden you don't like, why not clear it, instead of confining a variegated plant to the area? As someone who wants nothing to do with variegated cultivars, I used to believe mottled plants just came that way, and that people accepted all that unhealthy-looking foliage because the plants had other qualities. I was wrong—the people buying variegated varieties simply find plants with uniformly coloured leaves too boring.

Back to *Houttuynia cordata.* Does the variegated version also produce the same compounds that make its non-piebald cousin so interesting? And if so, which chemotype is it most like? You could of course find all this out yourself by buying a variegated plant and one each of the Japanese and Chinese varieties, cultivating all of them under the same conditions, and then setting up a little laboratory with a gas chromatograph in your bathroom. But if you just want to get your hands on a sleek, attractive green plant that makes healthy tea, you have to buy it from one of the few suppliers selling non-variegated *Houttuynia*—and then wait to see whether you get the Japanese or the Chinese chemotype. I got the latter.

Persicaria filiformis

Equipped with a satisfyingly sprawling *Houttuynia,* I went in search of the next plant. The first hurdle was to figure out exactly what kind of plant I was looking for. In Japan, it grows wild along roadways and cultivated in flower pots, and has tiny red flowers that line the stem, much like a strand of pearls. From a distance, it looks like shrubbery (if it is growing in clusters along a road) or it is practically invisible (when it is the only plant in a flowerpot); the beauty of this particular plant is only apparent on close inspection. This fact, as well as the lobe-like inflorescences, suggests knotweed. In the field of botany, it is sometimes possible to identify a plant by combining its most obvious characteristics into a name. And so this plant, with its threadlike flower arrangement, is known as the filamentous knotweed, *Persicaria filiformis.*

In a city that intentionally plants black locusts along the roads (for which I am regularly grateful in late spring, when the white butterfly-shaped blossoms give off their wonderful scent), I don't feel bad about planting a rampantly growing non-native knotweed in my planter. It can't be any worse than Japanese knotweed—which, incidentally, was brought here by Mr. von Siebold,[i] whose name commonly appears as the epithet in the botanical name of many plants native to Japan!

But finding one was no easy task. First, all suppliers act as though *Persicaria filiformis* and *Persicaria virginiana* are the same species. And second, a realization that should have occurred to me earlier: plants with flowers that are smaller than five millimetres are too boring for Germans, if they don't have variegated leaves. Which is why they peddle not just strange creations like *Persicaria virginiana*, but also varietals with descriptive names like Painter's Palette. It's enough to make you want to pull your hair out! That's how you make knotweed look like shrubbery from a distance—and from up close, too.

For the sake of accuracy, I should note that there is also species-specific variegation, which is not usually patchy-looking, nor is it detrimental to the plant. Instead, it can be functional and is often attractive, which is why, in that case, it would be less absurd to consider it a foliage plant. Knotweed leaves have naturally V-shaped dark red markings that are so pretty it's hard to understand why someone would prefer the plant with mottled leaves. Aren't most plants the most beautiful in their natural forms? Of course, it's understandable for growers to try for bigger and more spectacular flowers—and once you've been bitten by the bug, you probably don't want to do anything but crossbreed plants. But in most cases, I cannot understand why others are so keen on the results of this kind of breeding.

---

i The doctor and botanist Philipp Franz von Siebold was born in Würzburg and spent several years in Japan in the nineteenth century; at the time, the country was, to a great extent, still isolated from the West. The Japanese perennial knotweed, Fallopia japonica, which he brought to the Netherlands, counts among the most feared invasive plant species. Incidentally, knotweed owes its Latin name to Maarten Hottuyn, after whom the Houttuynia was named.

One of the few exceptions is the double-flowering liver-wort cultivar, which is pink instead of the usual purple. Compared to the Rubra plena version of *Hepatica nobilis,* the natural flowers look like veritable shrunken livers. Because the liverwort, small and modest, ekes out an inconspicuous existence in the undergrowth, I have no issue with it being a bit more luscious and bright. However, this pink, double-flowering *Hepatica*'s heyday is long past. As far back as the late 1800s, German naturalist and collector Carl August Bolle declared it an old-fashioned plant when he wrote the following about the liverwort: "The truly charming red double-flowering variety has become quite rare and can be considered particularly old-fashioned; the double-flowering blue variety is even harder to find."[ii] That's why nowadays—

[ii] Bolle's comments on the double-flowering liverwort are often quoted, probably because those who occupy themselves with topics such as these will sooner or later reach for the book by Heinz-Dieter Krausch, Kaiserkron und Päonien rot...[3], where they will find this wonderful quote, which is so irresistible, that they would also like to use it. Very illuminating—but less frequently quoted—are the following words by Bolle about "old-fashioned flowers" in general: "We encounter you on grass-covered churchyards, and also, at times, growing rampant along castle ruins or moss-covered monastery walls; yes, we might even, however rarely, unexpectedly come across you in the hustle and bustle of a big city, concealed behind forgotten planks. You are reluctant to give up customary locations. However, where we would search for you in vain would be the neatly manicured modern-day gardens where gravel-strewn pathways stand in contrast to carpet bedding flaunting glaringly bright scarlet geraniums. You might return here one time, at most, through the hands of fate, whose whims are satiated by the most modern fuchsia and begonias, recollecting Grandmother's musk hyacinth."[4] What is interesting here is the mildly disrespectful reference to those plants that are seemingly still favourites, particularly for balconies and as border plants, namely the beloved geranium (or pelargonium) and begonia (whereby it is important to note that there are very grandiose begonias—ones you will most likely never see on a balcony).

more than one hundred years later—you have to dig deep into your pockets to purchase one of these outmoded plants. Not just because they're rare, but as a rule, they can only be vegetatively propagated, meaning that, depending on the variety, a special *Hepatica* can easily cost one hundred euros in Germany. I question whether any pleasure can be had from owning such an expensive plant. You'd probably worry—more so than with any other favourite plant—that some harm might come to it.

Right now, I'm sheltering an *anemonopsis* that has actually budded, and I'm constantly worried that some clumsy lout will come too close and damage it. What's noteworthy here is that it's hard to get your hands on an *anemonopsis*. Even though I came across it in an antique magazine, the *anemonopsis* is not old-fashioned, but inexplicably has never been fashionable. Unfortunately, nobody carried it, and if they did list it, it was out of stock. So I tried seeds, which unfortunately wouldn't germinate. Finally, two years ago, I got my hands on one at a perennial plant market, but it didn't come back in the spring. Whether this was because it had been eaten by weevils or had suffered a late frost, I have no idea. Something killed my *anemonopsis*. Its replacement, purchased at the same periodically recurring market, has now developed buds and, aware of its transience, I'm fretting more over this one than its predecessor.

But back to the knotweed. I grudgingly ordered *Persicaria virginiana*, without splotches, and what did I get? *Persicaria amplexicaule*. Whatever. So I was still without *mizuhiki*, as the plant is called in Japanese, named after a paper cord that's used to decorate cards and gifts, as well as to make woven sculptures. And I've lost my desire to own a threaded knotweed—the likelihood of getting the wrong plant again was too much for me.

At least this won't happen when it comes to *Polytrichum*, simply because nobody supplies mosses. Under the erroneous assumption that common haircap moss was legally protected, I first planned to buy some. Because I suspected that scouring perennial nurseries would, in this case, be futile, I searched the internet to see what moss I could buy. This was a sobering undertaking. All manner of things, and even plants, are sold as moss, but in most cases, the goods on sale are not moss.[iii] And what I saw more of even than non-mosses, were anti-moss products and practices intended to get rid of moss. Demossing (not to be confused

---

iii The main non-mosses that are sold as moss are Sangina subulata or pearlwort, commonly known as Irish moss and which is in the Pink family; moss balls,* a species of green algae, Aegagropila linnaei, which grows into a ball-shaped orb and is often used for display purposes in aquarium tanks; and various types of lichen, a symbiosis of fungi and algae. To name a few: Cetraria islandica, or Iceland moss, used as a medicinal product; Evernia prunastri, oak moss, which, when used in perfume, forms the base note of many fragrances; and the various types of Cladonia, commonly used as "moss" in crafts for flower arrangements and, recently, sold for use as "moss walls."

*The term *moss ball*, in addition to describing the ball-shaped algae, also denotes a form of Japanese garden art whereby a substrate that is shaped into an orb is wrapped in moss; the balls are then either hung up somewhere or placed in a planter, either inside or outdoors. The popularity of these balls is evidenced by the fact that the base structures used to make them can be found in one-hundred-yen shops, the Japanese equivalent to the North American dollar store. However, they smell so strongly of pesticides (just as many of the stores do) that my inner aphid is filled with horror.

with harmless air layering)[iv] is a big topic unto itself. Moss is highly unpopular, especially in lawns—even less popular than mowing the lawn (which is very unpopular), but which could be avoided if people replaced their lawns entirely with moss. However, this obvious conclusion is reached only by a few outliers, most of whom wonder whether they dare go that route, since, according to popular opinion, moss is bad. But what's so bad about having moss in your lawn?

First, moss supposedly deprives grass of water and space to grow. Then it is condemned for not being robust, because it has no roots (you have to wonder why people have a problem with something dying if they don't want it in the first place—but in the end, they're probably just afraid of having "holes" in their lawn). That's a worthwhile argument if you want to play soccer on your lawn. Just like the assertion that wet moss is more slippery than wet grass. But none of this explains why people feel the need to remove moss from the cracks between their patio stones. Who wants to play soccer on a patio? Nobody wants to plant grass in the cracks between their patio stones. No, the moss has to go so you can see the brown earth between the patio slabs! But why? Are strips of soil more attractive than soft green beads of moss? No! But moss in the gaps can leave the impression of neglect, much like untrimmed nostril hairs, an unmowed lawn, or a dirty car. It's the fear of disorder, and nature. Or, to be more precise: a fear of the orderliness of nature—the fear of death. By conquering nature, people think they can

---

iv While some people try to eradicate it from their lawns, moss is also one of the key components in a gentle plant propagation method called air-layering, used in bonsai cultivation. As part of this process, a ring of bark is removed from the offshoot of the plant you wish to separate from the main plant later on. The resulting wound is wrapped in moss, which is bactericidal and fungicidal, keeping the damaged area from drying out. Once roots have developed on the treated area, the offshoot in question can be fully removed from the main plant and placed in soil or another suitable substrate.

outrun it. That moss, of all things—even more so than equally reviled so-called weeds—is often equated with neglect might be due to the fact that, through the way it spreads and its comparatively modest habitat requirements (it happily populates brickwork, for example), it becomes very obvious when things are less cared for than might be expected. There are enough buildings that would benefit from a little moss. In general, one can assume that moss protects the ground it grows on, instead of damaging it. Its antibacterial and antifungal properties are well known.

Nevertheless, moss is and often remains suspect by those who should, for myriad reasons, love it. Maybe it's because being rootless is fundamentally foreign to most people. To start with (or maybe it all ends here), there are no German names for most types of moss. This is a clear indication that moss is hardly of any interest to anyone. The same is true for most ferns and lichens. The only exceptions are the very common varieties, the particularly strange varieties, or those that have been used in one way or another. Mosses do not appear in most plant identification books (these are usually reserved for greater plants, even if their flowers are green and inconspicuous), and they are definitely not in books about plant care. With one exception: books about bonsai cannot manage without mentioning moss.

And so it's no coincidence that I discovered all these nondescript plants in Japan, or, more precisely, in Japanese gardens and flowerpots.[v] There are unassuming plants

---

v   The sidewalks in front of many houses in Japan—especially in the cities— are graced with potted plants that can absolutely be considered garden replacements. Particularly along quieter, smaller streets, there is no space for a garden around the houses, and the plant-friendly weather, as well as the low risk of theft, make it ideal for placing plants outside the front door. In these more or less large flowerpot conglomerates, the ratio of so-called green plants to those with striking flowers is similar to what is seen in the average Japanese garden.

in fields and in forests throughout the world, but most don't end up being cultivated without being unadulterated if, upon closer inspection, they have no further obvious use beyond their beauty. There are several reasons this is different in Japan. One of them is probably just paying more attention to detail. This turns bland knotweed threads into ornamental cords, and moss, supposedly capable of displacing a lawn, into a little forest,[vi] if not a whole world.[vii] This sense of hyperfocus while dismissing or ignoring larger issues is conducive to a quiet life, and makes it easier to isolate while living in a densely populated island city constantly under threat from above (typhoons), below (earthquakes), and all sides (tsunamis). Anyone who can overlook their neighbours' fighting and remain calm despite ever-looming meteorological or geological calamity is surely also able to look past even the most lush shrubbery to perceive the smallest red-and-white flowers as stars resembling the light reflected by dewdrops.

A second—and probably the most important—reason is that the traditional Japanese garden represents an idealized landscape, one that is more (as for example, in the *Karesansui*, the Japanese rock garden, often called a Zen garden) or less stylized. But one thing that does not belong in a landscape—particularly not in an ideal one—is a geometric arrangement of large-flowered plants reminiscent of a military formation. These flowerbeds look like military troops that have come to a standstill. Baroque gardens look so unnatural and rigid that one has to wonder why designers didn't simply create stone

---

vi In Japanese, juniper haircap moss is called sugigoke; sugi is the word for the so-called Japanese cedar, which is a conifer in the cypress family, Cryptomeria. There is therefore agreement that this moss looks like a cypress plant.

vii On this note, I recommend the chapter "In the Forest of the Waterbear" in Gathering Moss by Robin Wall Kimmerer.[5]

mosaics instead. But perhaps the obvious conquest of nature belongs to the ongoing demonstration of power by these gardens. Of course, Europeans no longer put in Baroque gardens, but they still tend toward flowers (particularly when planting in public spaces) and clearly delimited beds.

It goes without saying that nature is the subject of a Japanese garden, it's just less visible. The wonderfully gnarled pine trees don't become so perfectly windswept on their own—a gardener has to come a few times a year to prune them into their seemingly unspoiled form. That gentle mound over there? It was created with fill. And of course the plants standing over there seemingly by chance don't grow there naturally, and of course weren't planted there by chance, either. It still feels like you're in paradise. But even if, in a paradise such as this, moss and other inconspicuous plants are more welcome than they are in a pompous parade of big blooms, we shouldn't falsely conclude that people are responsible for all Japan's mossy beauty. The garden of Saihhō-ji became a moss garden—one of the most famous in the world—because nobody took care of it. This isn't so unusual—in *The Gardens of Japan* by Jiro Harada there are illustrations of the northeast garden of Daisen-in,[viii] [6] which is so overgrown with moss that you can no longer see the gravel surrounding the carefully placed rocks. The moss has since been removed,[ix] and the gravel has been neatly raked back in place against a small, rebuilt wall. What's remarkable is that the moss in the Saihō-ji garden and other temples hasn't been removed.

The *Yamakei Color Guide Kyoto* from 1968 sums this up: "The garden [...] of Saihō-ji has not been kept well and the

---

[viii] Daisen-in is a sub-temple of Daitoku-ji in Kyoto. Its rock gardens are some of the most well-known examples of karesansui, or dry landscape style.

[ix] There is still a little bit. Behind the rocks, in front of the (rebuilt) wall, a bit of moss was left on the gravel.

ground is overrun with moss. However, the beautiful moss has won the fame. The ruin has beauty. Nothing is permanent. This is Zen thought."[7]

In contrast with the Saihhō-ji garden, tea gardens are literally designed for moss growth. The tea garden serves as a pathway to the tea house; in Japanese, this small garden is called a roji (露地), which literally translates as *dewy path*. The experience of walking through the tea garden serves, so to speak, as preparation for the tea ceremony. In *The Book of Tea*, Okakura Kakuzhō describes it as follows:

> The roji was intended to break connection with the outside world and to produce a fresh sensation conducive to the full enjoyment of aestheticism in the tea room itself. One who has trodden this garden path cannot fail to remember how his spirit, as he walked in the twilight of evergreens over the regular irregularities of the stepping stones, beneath which lay dried pine needles, and passed beside the moss-covered granite lanterns, became uplifted above ordinary thoughts. One may be in the midst of a city and yet feel as if he were in the forest far away from the dust and din of civilization.[8]

The plants that must be present in a tea garden and those that have no place there are strictly regulated.[x] A sunflower would be as foreign to a roji as a UFO, and without moss, the garden would be missing an essential component. Moss is so central to a roji that one cannot help but wonder whether the stepping stones are there to protect the guests' feet from the (damp) moss or to protect the moss from the guests' feet. Jiro

---

[x] Plants that are appropriate to a tea garden include mosses, ferns, and evergreen trees and shrubs. Conspicuously flowering plants such as hortensias and azaleas are not planted in these gardens, or only very sparingly.[12]

Harada writes about these stones: "The height takes into consideration the growth of moss on the ground and also pine needles with which the ground is covered in order to protect the moss or the ground against frost."[9]

Moss embodies two aesthetic principles that are closely tied to the tea ceremony and are usually spoken in one breath: *wabi* and *sabi.* The term *wabi* encompasses a concept that cannot be translated with one word alone. Daisetz Teitaro Suzuki describes it in his book, *Zen and Japanese Culture,* as follows:

> Stated in terms of practical everyday life, wabi is to be satisfied with a little hut, a room of two or three *tatami* (mats), like the log cabin of Thoreau's log cabin, and with a dish of vegetables picked in the neighbouring fields, and maybe listening to the pattering of a gentle spring rainfall.[10]

Teiji Itoh summarizes this as "tranquil simplicity." *Sabi* is similar; by way of an explanation, Itoh describes it using the phrase "patina of age."[11] Moss embodies both principles simultaneously. Although it is only sabi indirectly, as it always gives an impression of being young and fresh, it covers the surface, or the substrate, on which it grows with a patina. Teiji Itoh writes:

> Indeed, sabi is at its ultimate when age and wear bring a thing to the very threshold of its demise. Appreciation of sabi confirms the natural cycle of organic life— that what is created from the earth finally returns to the earth and that nothing is ever complete. Sabi is true to the natural cycle of birth and rebirth.[13]

Seen this way, the moss in the tea garden is valued for the very reason people want to drive it out from the cracks between their patio stones. How does such diametrical opposition come about? In Jun'ichirhō Tanizaki's *In Praise of Shadows*, the author explains the very disparate appreciation of light and shadow in the West and the East, which might even illuminate the possible reasons for such highly divergent perceptions:

> We fill our gardens with dense paintings, they spread out a flat expanse of grass. But what produces such differences in taste? In my opinion it is this: we [Asians] tend to seek our satisfactions in whatever surroundings we happen to find ourselves, to content ourselves with things as they are; and so darkness causes us no discontent, we resign ourselves to it as inevitable. If light is scarce then light is scarce; we will immerse ourselves in the darkness and there discover its own particular beauty.[14]

Even if you're a fan of bright lights, after reading Tanizaki's essay, you're left with the desire to unscrew every single light bulb. Just like how, after visiting Japan, you want a bit more moss back home. Like in Southern France, where there are moss-covered fountains. These fountains haven't been cleaned up or restored, and thus over time, have transformed into enchanted green lumps. No one is gardening there; this is all about the art of laissez-faire. There are moss fountains like this in Italy, too, and they could exist in Germany as well, if people stopped removing the moss. Moss grows undeniably well in this country; otherwise people wouldn't get so upset about it.

Now, in all fairness, I shouldn't fail to mention that things have gotten better when it comes to moss acceptance in Germany. Moss has almost become a bit hip. Companies are selling panels that you can use to cover surfaces with moss—supposedly. They're actually covered in lichen, *Cladonia*. The lichen is chemically treated to remain flexible and deflect dirt, and it's dyed to a desirable shade of green, because moss is green and lichen is more of a whitish pale green that looks like it could glow in the dark. Admittedly, it looks very chic and feels rather nice, but do you really want to hang chemically treated, dyed[xi] lichen in your apartment? Probably not, and most definitely not once you learn that lichens only grow a few millimetres every year, and feed reindeer in the winter months. Furthermore, don't forget that these delicate tundra inhabitants use photosynthesis—some types even do so at sub-zero temperatures. The role they play in maintaining our climate is not a minor one. Besides, a panel covered with clusters of lichen—won't that collect dust? How on earth would you get the dust off the textured surface? No, I don't get it. Why reach for lichen when every so often a magpie pulls a moss tuft out of the eavestrough that you can plant into an old cup and keep alive? Or you can wait until liverwort takes root in a flowerpot outside your door and creates its own little landscape that looks straight out of a 1960s science-fiction film, with its thalloid terraces, porous gemma cups, and the antheridia and archegonia, which look like they could be used to send classified information into space.

On top of that, extract of *Marchantia* is said to repel a creature that's just as unpopular among gardeners as the weevil: the Spanish slug. This might lead to liverwort outranking even the common green lacewing[xii] as the most desired plant protector in all of Europe.

---

xi In this case, the "chemical" is a salt solution, presumably harmless. Likely more harmless than the dye used to colour the lichen. And more harmless than the glue used to attach the lichen to the panel. Which is probably not made of cardboard.

xii The common green lacewing, Chrysoperla carnea, is a beautiful, triangular green insect that belongs to the lacewing family. Their larvae, so-called aphid lions, like to eat, among others, mites and—the name says it all—aphids. They are such perfect "pest" destroyers that they are sold as beneficial organisms. It is said that they like the vermilion plant and catnip.

The fact that these moss panels are finding buyers at all demonstrates a longing for the green spaces nature offers the eye, not just for colourful flowers. Day-to-day city life is so bright and stimulating that it's not surprising citizens yearn for more than a taste of nature; they want a whole forest. A little cushion of haircap moss is much better at bringing a hint of woodland solitude into a city garden than a throng of Franz Kafka pompom dahlias, no matter how beautiful they may be. Sinking into a moss's lush, absorbent green is like sinking into a soft mattress.

A friend brought me a cushion of haircap moss from the forest; it now lives beside my *Houttuynia*. They get along famously—same with the maiden hair fern and the Gray's sedge. The *anemonopsis* died. This year, I couldn't find a replacement at the perennial market—instead, I finally found a knotweed.

Roberta Schneider lives in winter hardiness zone 8a, collects Araceae and Zingiberaceae, works as an author and a translator, and enjoys jumping from one topic of conversation to another. She doesn't trust people who are more scared of big spiders than big cars and who are more frightened of moss in their gardens than herbicides.

1 Lafcadio Hearn, "In a Japanese Garden," in Atlantic Monthly 70 (417) (Boston: July 1892).

2 Carl August Bolle, "Altmodische Blumen" [Old-Fashioned Flowers], in Brandenburgia 8 (Berlin: P. Stankiewicz' Buchdruckerei, 1900), 196.

3 Heinz-Dieter Krausch, Kaiserkron und Päonien rot...Entdeckung und Einführung unserer Gartenblumen [Red crown imperials and peonies...Exploring and introduction to flowers in our gardens], (Hamburg: Dölling & Galitz Verlag, 2003).

4 Carl August Bolle, "Altmodische Blumen" [Old-Fashioned Flowers], in Brandenburgia 8 (Berlin: P. Stankiewicz' Buchdruckerei, 1900), 185–86.

5 Robin Wall Kimmerer, Gathering Moss—A Natural and Cultural History of Mosses (Oregon: Oregon University Press, 2003).

6 Jiro Harada, The Gardens of Japan (London: The Studio Limited, 1928), 49 and 128.

7 Keiichi Tsukamoto, Masanobu Mitsuaki Karā Kyoto (Tokyo: Yama-to-keikoku Sha, 1968), 55.

8 Okakura Kakuzō, The Book of Tea (New York: Duffield and Company, 1919), 82-83.

9 Jiro Harada, 29.

10 Daisetz Teitaro Suzuki, Zen and Japanese Culture (New York: Pantheon Books, 1959), 23.

11 Teiji Itoh, Wabi Sabi Suki (Tokyo: Cosmo Public Relation Corp.; publ. Hiroshima: Mazda Motor Corporation, 1993), 7.

12 See Karl Hennig, Japanische Gartenkunst [Japanese Garden Art] (Cologne: DuMont, 1980).

13 Teiji Itoh, 7.

14 Jun'ichirō Tanizaki, In Praise of Shadows, trans. Thomas J. Harper and Edward G. Seidensticker [1933] (London: Jonathan Cape, 1991), 47.

ANNETTE HOLLÄNDER

Planting, Saving, and Propagating Heirloom Vegetables

Those who grow their own vegetables know the joys of eating freshly harvested lettuce or sun-warmed tomatoes. Growing vegetables goes hand in hand with a love of eating well and a love of high-quality ingredients. At the same time, working in the garden offers balance, energy, and satisfaction.

I've been passionate about gardening since I was a child, even though I haven't always been able to indulge in it. Because we grew up in the country, it was natural to cultivate a vegetable garden and to nourish ourselves with its produce.

Over the years, and with the right life partner, we've now created a garden from which we can sustain ourselves with vegetables year-round. Additionally, we're maintaining a preservation repository for heirloom and endangered vegetable varieties.

The Path to Heirloom Vegetables

It was a desire to grow flavourful specialities and to extend the harvest period in our garden as long as possible that led me to so-called heirloom vegetable varieties. At the same time, we developed a deep appreciation for our cultivars and came to understand how gardeners and cultivars form a symbiotic relationship: while the plants feed us, many cultivars also need the gardener to enable them to survive in their cultivated form.

If we look at the work of the gardener in this interplay, we might very well ask who chose whom. Have people chosen a plant for its benefit and nourishment or have plants chosen people to benefit from their cultivation and propagation efforts?

Apart from such thoughts, the variety of available cultivars, of vegetables in all imaginable colours and shapes, is unbelievably fascinating. Once you start to study the field, you'll discover there's virtually no limit to the number of enticing rarities. And so, every year, we are spoiled for choice when it comes to selecting our seeds.

I've established favourite vegetables, ones I have no desire to do without either in my garden or on my plate. They include, among others, purple broccoli for the first spring harvest, wonderful eggplants that are suitable for planting outdoors, fleshy giant sugar snap peas, yellow Anellino di Trento bush beans, a blue pointed cabbage that makes the best coleslaw, and of course a beautiful selection of colourful tomatoes, with all their different flavours, and so on. But we're also trying out new heirloom varieties every year, some of which earn a steady place in our vegetable patch for the long term.

In Search of Good Heirloom Varieties

Many of these heirloom varieties have a lot to offer, both for kitchen gardens and in terms of self-sufficiency. An important property is their robustness for outdoor cultivation. After all, they came into existence at a time when heated greenhouses and imported vegetables were still a long way off. Their oft-associated winter hardiness ensures a longer harvest season, and many of these vegetables also offer a striking appearance and noteworthy flavour experience at the same time.

Most of these vegetable varieties are rarely available in grocery stores. Tomatoes are a case in point: many of the different tomato varieties that taste great have very thin skins. As a rule, they're not available in grocery stores because they neither transport nor store well, and this makes them unsuitable for commercial production. The same is true of many other heirloom vegetables. They also might not adhere to uniform, standardized vegetable sizing, or their harvest yield is prioritized over flavour.

Even when it comes to purchasing seeds, the search for colourful heirloom vegetable varieties is often in vain. Seed companies carry the same standard selection as grocery stores. Tomatoes are red, cucumbers are green, and eggplants are aubergine. That there are other options—never mind the fact that the available options were once very different—is something very few people know, be they gardeners or consumers. And the few exceptions, such as yellow tomatoes or purple so-called heirloom carrots, show themselves to not really be older varieties, on closer inspection.

So where do you find heirloom vegetables? I originally obtained many of my favourite varieties from seed banks or private growers. Fortunately, the group of people propagating and offering heirloom seeds is gradually expanding. In recent years, seed events have sprouted in many locations, and these are great places to find heirloom seeds.

However, if you really want to cultivate these treasured vegetables from year to year, the best option is to propagate a plant in your own garden. After all, you never know if you'll be able to find seeds for any given variety in the coming years.

By acquiring and growing these rarities, as well as collecting your own seeds, you get to enjoy delicious vegetables and at the same time contribute to their preservation. After all, a vegetable variety won't go extinct as long as we continue to grow, eat, and propagate it.

Crop-Bearing Plant Diversity Is in Danger of Becoming Extinct

Now, of course, the question arises as to why these heirloom vegetable varieties aren't available in stores. It's worth taking a look back at the history of our seeds.

Over a long period of development—from when humans first started to intentionally grow food for eating to current plant breeding techniques—an unbelievably large variety of cultivars emerged. Cultivation and propagation occurred primarily in the hands of farmers. Many of these so-called heirloom varieties were adapted to the climate and soil conditions of the regions in which they came to be grown. It was customary for farmers to grow their own crop-bearing plants and to exchange seeds; this ensured their survival, as well as the diversity of the crops.

Nowadays, the cultivation of plants for use as food and for the production of seeds is kept separate. Seeds must be purchased for farming; horticultural and home gardening are subject to very strict seed legislation. Seeds from varieties that are not officially authorized can't be sold. Authorized varieties are not only subject to strict criteria, but the associated costs are also very high. Garden centres and smaller seed companies cannot afford these permits.

At the same time, modern plant breeding is mainly geared toward hybrid breeding for industrial farming. The breeding goals here are maximum yields and turbo growth, mechanical processability, transportability, and shelf life, as well as a visually uniform appearance. Many of the older regional and farm varieties do not meet these requirements. And their diversity—fruit, heads, and tubers that are not always the same size and shape—has long been considered undesirable.

This has resulted in a wide-scale loss of the older varieties. According to estimates, we've lost about 75 percent of our arable crops since 1900.

Old Vegetable Varieties Are Open Pollinated

The old vegetable varieties were bred for specific properties over a period of many years through cross-breeding and careful selection. These properties included colour, flavour, shape, resistance, etc. If these varieties are propagated using seed, the next generation of plants will have those same properties—this is referred to as open pollination and is reproducible. Before modern plant breeding gained in significance, this was the way to breed new varieties or further develop existing varieties.

Seeds designated as F1, on the other hand, are hybrid seeds that are either sterile or don't breed true. The term F1 designates the first generation of a cross-pollinated plant and stands for Filial 1. Two pure varietal lines are crossed, resulting in highly uniform first-generation offspring. F1 breeding takes advantage of this uniformity.

However, if these plants are further propagated, the next generation—F2—will exhibit the greatest possible genetic disparity, and many variations of the cross partner's genetic properties will appear in the offspring. It is therefore not possible to propagate F1 varieties to have the same properties as the original plants. This means that seeds of a certain variety have to be repurchased every year.

Adaptation and Climate Change

It is precisely the (no longer desired) genetic diversity of an open-pollinated variety that allows it to adapt to changed growing conditions. At one time, plants would adapt to their regional conditions, and in times of climate change, this ability is more than worth considering, given the basis of our food supply. Locally adapted, open-pollinated crop-bearing plants often have good horizontal resistance, making it possible to grow them without pesticides or chemical fertilizers.

Depending on the region in which they are grown, they can be resistant to drought, heat, or cold. They are therefore made for setting the course for our urgently needed shift toward sustainable, organic agriculture and farming practices.

Plant Breeders and Seed Companies

In a not-so-distant past, countless breeders shared in the seed market; now there are only a few multinational seed companies. At present, 75 percent of the global seed market is held by ten international corporations. And that concentration continues to gain momentum. Small breeding businesses can no longer compete and are being bought up by the corporate giants.

The older breeders were closely connected to their breeding. The names of the varieties reflect the pride and devotion they felt toward the cultivars they'd created. Queens and kings, beauties and miracles, and even the names of the breeders were bestowed upon new varieties.

Modern seed corporations work with state-of-the-art breeding technology, including genetic engineering. It is therefore not uncommon to see the creation of inbred lines and manipulations at the cellular level in order to achieve a desired breeding goal. Breeding must be profitable: there is no room for feelings toward vegetable plants. Assembly line products are being created; not even sterile strains that can no longer propagate can stop them. It's been said that plant creations like these lose parts of their soul. Even if you forgo a spiritual perspective, the development of crop-bearing plant breeding and the industrial seed market is problematic.

Throughout the world, non-reproducible seeds and crops that are subject to licence fees are depriving more and more small-scale farmers of their traditional ways of life. They are not only being driven into dependency, but all too often into giving up their farmland, into poverty, or even to suicide.

Is Gardening a Private Matter?

In light of these developments, gardening—especially when it comes to vegetables—is no longer really a private matter. Every home gardener cultivates their personal preferences in their garden. But every seed envelope and every plant purchased supports either seed corporations and their breeding and marketing methods, or preserves our old, open-pollinated vegetable varieties.

Ultimately, this decline in crop diversity signifies the loss of a cultural heritage that has evolved over a thousand years, and it represents a threat to one of our most important livelihoods. With this in mind, my wish for all of us is a future where many fields and gardens are once again home to an inspiring variety of strong and thriving plants.

The deep desire to work with and for nature is what prompted **Annette Holländer**, a qualified colour lithography specialist and media designer, to take a new professional path after working for many years in the publishing and online industry. Through her training in growing seeds and outdoor education, she acquired the fundamentals required to conserve our cultivars and conduct educational activities. She currently provides workshops and gives talks on growing seeds, crop-bearing plant diversity, and how to maintain a self-sufficient organic garden. Through tasting sessions, she provides insight into the delicious diversity of heritage vegetable varieties. In addition, she runs school gardening projects and leads classroom programs in which children learn to grow seasonal and regional food, and learn about a wide variety of topics around nature and the environment. She shares seeds from the heritage and special open-pollinated vegetable varieties that she grows and propagates in her garden to interested home gardeners for personal use. Seed offers, descriptions of plant varieties, recipes, and much more can be found at www.garten-des-lebens.de.

1   Vandana Shiva, scientist and environmental activist, has conducted studies that show the impacts of genetically modified seeds on farmers: www.vandanashiva.com.

ELKE VON RADZIEWSKY

Gardening in Tune with Nature

1. ROB LEOPOLD'S SEED LIST

The rain has been coming down in buckets for days, weeks. Rob and Antje Leopold's cottage is tucked into the heart of the flat countryside of the Netherlands, near Groningen. The flowers of the love-in-a-mist in front of the windows hang their heads. Chickweed and nettle are brimming with vitality, and they don't mind the wet month of June in the least. In that summer of 1993, Rob Leopold did what every gardener feels like doing when faced with such a discouraging situation. He hung his rake in the tree, left his shovel in the ground, and quit. Let whatever grows grow: nettles, plantain, maybe a marsh orchid, a terrestrial orchid in front of simple rushes—what florist could come up with a better arrangement? It was all good.

Later, he said he felt "like a ripe apple that had dropped to the grass" and was then brought into the house, because even inside, the garden was an endless topic for him. He continued gardening at his desk.[1] Not in the form of borders and beds, but in the form of paragraphs and pages. Row by row, he enjoyed the image of a writer being like a gardener. Rob Leopold was the engine, the craftsman, the public relations person, and the pioneer of the Dutch garden movement that, since the 1980s, has brought more and more Germans, Brits, and Swedes to Holland to see what's happening in their gardens.

He was passionate, with bottomless enthusiasm, regardless of whether his mind, his hands, or his gardens were filled with flowers—or the wild seeds on the table in front of him that he distributed. He was a salesman. Or an expert in the field of natural gardening. He was the leader behind a theory of gardening in tune with nature. He preferred to see himself as the first independent garden philosopher.

Bringing the Countryside to the House

Almost every child knows that tomatoes and sunflowers are mass-produced in Holland, fuelled by nutrient solutions, under artificial light, in wind-protected spaces. Travellers to the country, whether now or forty years ago, get the impression that half the country is under glass, erected for the cultivation of supermarket vegetables. And where there are no reflective panes of glass, in May blooming tulips cover the ground, sorted by the hectare into a patchwork of red, yellow, and white.

The garden movement that came to Germany in the 1980s in response to the mighty plant industry hasn't been called the Dutch Wave for a while now, but it can still be mentioned in the same breath as the New German Garden Style (the best-known example is the Hermannshof in Weinheim, Germany, which was first maintained by Urs Walser, now by Cassian Schmidt)—and the New American Style, which has existed in this canon since the High Line became New York's number one tourist attraction.

Its focus is on the portion of nature present in a garden, or a garden's "naturalness"—an idea that ran like a thread throughout the twentieth century, arising here and there, following no apparent logic, and which was rarely without opposition. In Switzerland, Eduard Neuenschwander (1924–2013) defined the gardener as nature's social worker, leading Dieter Kienast (1945–98) to publish his polemic against the eco-kitsch on garage roofs. In France, Gilles

Clément (born in 1943) worked on his idea of the garden in movement and introduced it in the celebrated Parisian Parc André-Citroën alongside Allain Provost's (born in 1938) austere architectural garden. In Germany, the memory of influential designers such as Otto Valentien (1897–1987), Wilhelm Hübotter (1895–1976), and Adolf Haag (1903–66; Gustav Lange, who designed the Berlin Mauerpark, studied under him) was suppressed; before, during, and after the Third Reich, they designed gardens with the notion that the garden should "bring the countryside to the house using the simplest of means."[2] In 1938, Otto Valentien posited: "The gourmet among plant lovers prefers wild perennials over their overbred variations." But they hadn't forgotten the landscape architect Willy Lange (1864–1941), who goes back one more generation, and his teachings from *Naturbildern im Garten* (*Images of Nature in the Garden*), which, at the time, was ruthlessly declared by Hermann Muthesius as impractical and the "height of ridiculousness." And then there was Richard Hansen (1912–2001), who, as a student of field botanist and phytosociology pioneer Reinhold Tüxen (1899–1980; among others, consultant to Alwin Seifert in the design of the German autobahns built under the Third Reich), developed a gardening theory on the basis of grouping plants based on their natural habitats (1971, 1981). Too complicated to have any far-reaching impact, it's very scientific and erudite, and appeals to anyone who loves structure, theories, and systems.

Hippie, Salesman, Philosopher

For close to half a century, Rob Leopold wasn't one of those people whose life was rooted in the history of gardening. He was of the postwar generation, born in November 1949. At the age of fifteen, he read Camus and Sartre, watched the movie *Hiroshima, My Love*, and had the feeling that life was mocking him. "Love? Ridiculous in a world of concentration camps and atom bombs." Then came the sixties, and suddenly the world became a colourful place. Flower children put literal flowers in their hair, expanded their consciousness with mescaline and LSD, and travelled to Kathmandu. Freedom to the people, freedom to the plants. Seed bombs exploded in England's manicured parks. The Jackson 5 sang, "We can change the world."

To change the world, one person went to Peru to weave, another person dyed wool, and in Groningen, Rob Leopold ran a store for fabrics made from natural fibres, which he sourced from Thailand, India, and Nepal. He also started to look for forgotten plants. First it was plants that could be used for dyes, and then ancient medicinal plants, wild herbs, and vegetables. Founded in 1978, Rob's Cruydt-Hoeck company became the nucleus of his peaceful revolution; unique for its time, it sold seeds of wild plant species and, later on, select, refined varieties of annual and perennial flowers and grasses. Rob Leopold's trajectory through the 1970s took him from hippie to natural gardener.

In the eighties, he got to know Piet Oudolf, who later became the rock star of the Dutch Wave; he also met Romke van de Kaa, Henk Gerritsen, Harry Kramer, Coen Jansen and Ton ter Linden, and other people who were tied to the patch of earth on which they worked, whether as professional gardeners, plant breeders, or artists. Just like Leopold, they had a fresh vision of the garden: they experimented with natural plants and campaigned against the overly cultivated iris or larkspurs as decorative garden elements. Rob Leopold wanted to be their chronicler, their agent, and medium. He searched his country for special gardeners, or traditional gardeners, as they called themselves, exchanged ideas with them, published their addresses, filmed television movies, conspired with gardening book authors, organized symposiums, brought together gardeners and botanists. He was usually miles ahead of the orthodox countryside: kitchen garden plants, colourful flower meadows—he'd long tilled the fields while others were still sharpening their spades.

From the get-go, he kept a detailed record of the gardening movement, jotting down every conversation, every event in a journal. But his most powerful work as an independent garden philosopher was *de Dikke Zadenlijst* (*the Big Seed List*). It was the foundation, the material that formed the basis of new gardens and a text that fuelled others. It contained what Rob Leopold referred to as "real plants." He first tracked them down as names in old books, catalogues, and lists; then he tracked them down in botanical gardens, from plant breeders and collectors and wherever else possible. He sowed and tested them in the fields behind his home, described them, recommended them, and sold them through his *Big Seed List*.

The Stuff New Gardens Are Made Of

Ambrosiana mexicana, dainty, green, a metre tall, and offering an exotic hint of frankincense. *Nigella*, all varieties that ever existed and were considered beautiful. *Digitalis ferruginea*, the foxglove with the beige-coloured flowers and the brown-veined throat. Not delicate, but a proudly towering plant, one for those who like to stop and take a closer look. Just like parchment-coloured *Astrantia*, silvery *Artemisia*, copper-coloured bronze fennel: lots of wild-looking, sometimes fragrant plants in delicate palettes of different shades. Rob Leopold called these shades "gradients" and made them a pillar of his philosophy. To be able to see and understand nuances, and not have the senses overcome by the bright yellow of the overly fertilized petunia and the fire-engine red of Vulcan Red *Lobelia*, is to not follow the call of the masses. "Are road signs and billboards the only things that still draw our attention?" he asked. "Are we constantly driving through the countryside at a speed of a hundred kilometres per hour, blind to the elegance with which the blade of grass bends under the weight of a beetle?" The garden and its plants should teach us about life.

Anyone who spoke to him could feel how his heart overflowed. More than anything, he would have liked to embrace nature in its entirety. He babbled away like a brook, quavered like a poplar in the wind, got lost in Holland's endless meadows. He could not sit still while conversing; he jumped about and danced like a faun. His flow of speech was like water on a mill wheel. Did he long to finally escape the millstone, the speed of which was in opposition to his world view? This was the nineties. *Big Seed List* appeared for the last time in 1998, boasting nine hundred different species and varieties.

---

2. THE ROMKE VAN DE KAA MEADOW

Rob Leopold died in the early summer of 2005. For as long as he was there, he continued to drive the Dutch garden movement, trumpeting and organizing with his "we can change the world" view wherever he went. There was the group of traditional, fine gardeners with their ambitious, natural varieties who established Perennial Perspectives in 1992, an association of professionals who would meet and exchange ideas; in addition to gardeners, they included landscape architects from England, Germany, Sweden, and Holland. Rob Leopold was highly instrumental in the founding of this group. It still exists today, but its website no longer mentions its origins. The garden movement, at least the way it appeared through Rob Leopold's eyes, dried up with his death; maybe it was only there because he wanted it to be. If we were to ask one of the critical eyewitnesses from back then, Dutch gardener and garden author Romke van de Kaa, who ran in the same group, no garden movement originated in Holland.

The English Archetype, German Tradition

Romke van de Kaa studied biology, then psychology, and then in 1973, left academia and switched over to the holy land of horticulture, where he worked in Wisley, England, in one of the Royal Horticultural Society's four gardens. He met Beth Chatto, the famous pioneer of organic gardening. From 1975 to 1979, Romke was head gardener for England's furious garden icon, Christopher Lloyd, at his Great Dixter garden in East Sussex, located in Southern England; he then spent a year in Lismore, Ireland. With this first-class training, his many contacts, and an assortment of plants, he returned to Holland, met Piet Oudolf, and in 1981 they founded Hummelo, a garden centre that soon became known in Holland and beyond. Now it is considered a nucleus of the Dutch Wave, almost a kind of artist colony, much like Barbizon or Worpswede. Their collaboration only lasted until 1985. It was jealousy—in Romke's words, "Who is the most sought-after gardener in the country?"—that drove them apart.

For Romke van de Kaa, who had acquired his knowledge in England, and who, with Christopher Lloyd, had visited German avant-garde gardens like Munich's Westpark, with its perennial plantings by Rosemarie Weisse, the so-called Dutch Wave was nothing more than hype, nonsense. Years earlier, he'd gotten to know Christopher Lloyd and Beth Chatto (now in her nineties), natural gardeners whose work predated any Dutch Wave. Beth Chatto's books, in which she wrote about her gravel gardens that never needed watering, or her shade gardens, had made her a luminary beyond England's borders.

"Plants, like people," she argued, "have their preferences, and don't like being thrust into the nearest available hole." The question that a gardener needs to ask should always be: "What does the plant need?" Beth Chatto drew the gaze away from gaudy, pompous flowers to leaves and seed heads.[3]

Interesting note: to start Unusual Plants, the garden centre she founded in 1978, she bought plants from the Gräfin von Zeppelin perennials nursery. Located in Sulzburg, which is not far from Freiburg in Breisgau, this was one of Germany's leading nurseries at the time. Another interesting fact: her husband, Andrew, who helped her put in the garden, was, even if he couldn't read German, a follower of the phyto-sociology formulated by Reinhold Tüxen and then Richard Hansen, which advocates for gardening that is in tune with plants' natural habitats.[4]

Streamlined Gardening

After Romke van de Kaa left Hummelo, he founded a new garden centre in Dieren, just fifteen kilometres from Hummelo and not far from Apeldoorn. He wrote articles and books, became a popular columnist, and earned the reputation of being Holland's most relaxed gardener: "If you don't have time, let the garden do its thing. An overgrown garden is not a jungle or chaos. It's only streamlined gardening."

For thirteen years now, Romke van de Kaa has been experimenting with his big project, well off the beaten path forged by the Dutch Wave and New German Garden Style. It lies behind his small, ancient house, immediately in front of floor-to-ceiling windows: a meadow, unfolding as though on a stage. The land was a rubbish dump, and he had "a big machine come and flatten the whole thing." Blackberries, nettles, and thistles took over the plot. He mowed it for four years, "just like what you'd do if you're trying to put in a nice lawn."

In the fifth year, he started planting snowdrops and other flowering bulbs. From that point forward, he modified his mowing to be considerate of the plants' growth cycles, so as to not lose them again immediately. "I counted: six weeks from when the last daffodils bloom." This was usually June. A few years later, he added cranesbill and salvia. That pushed back the first date for mowing. Finally, he sowed various varieties of orchids, *Dactylorhiza*, and marsh orchids. Then it was August. A regular lawn mower wouldn't be able to cut the meadow plants, which were hardy and woody so late in the season. For that first late mowing, Romke van de Kaa now rents a special, heavy-duty mower every year. After this, he trundles his way through the meadow weekly, pauses while the fall crocuses bloom, and then shears the grasses one last time in November.

Nature's Screenplay

Romke van de Kaa's meadow is a continuous gardening process and a lesson in nature with respect to group dynamics, dependent on soil chemistry and specific plant and animal communities. He is always trying something new: "Some things don't even start growing, other things disappear over time." Seeding is a challenge. Grasses create shade the seedlings cannot compete with. Unless you take what the meadow has to offer: anthills and molehills. "Some plants, some violets, for example, will not grow in any other type of soil." Planting is better than seeding: bulbs, like *Fritillaria*, botanical tulips, *Tulipa sprengeri* and *clusiana*, allium, anemones, *Camassia*, as well as perennial cranesbill and salvia.

He also uses the survival strategies of hemiparasitic plants. Yellow-flowered *Rhinanthus*, commonly known as little yellow rattle, feeds from various meadow plants. Once it has eaten itself out of house and home, it moves on to the next strongest specimen. Withering grasses remain, among which wildflowers flourish.

To date, no two years of this meadow experiment have been alike. One summer, there was more sorrel than there had ever been, and along with it, songbirds: "Siskins, greenfinches, chaffinches, bramblings, goldfinches; I had no idea that there would be so many birds wanting to eat the rumex seeds." His binoculars within reach, a bird book in hand, van de Kaa sees the "planted" meadow as the opposite of an immobile shrub, tree, and flower photo: it is an outdoor cinema, a movie, and his involvement in the screenplay is ongoing.

3. PIET OUDOLF'S MATRIX

The trajectory followed by van de Kaa's former partner, Piet Oudolf, led him to the international design world. One of his first steps was to publish the book *Droomplanten* (*Dream Plants for the Natural Garden*) in the late nineties, which he produced together with Henk Gerritsen (1948 to 2008).[5] Gerritsen, like Rob Leopold, had a philosophical mind and was the founder of the famous Priona Tuinen gardens, in addition to being the designer behind Nicky and Strilli Oppenheimer's Waltham Place in Berkshire, England. Gerritsen formulated a theory of dreamed nature and gardening on the limits of total wilderness that could only be achieved and maintained by masters: "A garden such as this will not outlive its owner."[6] In other words, natural gardening is always an individual path.

The Good Plants Guide

Dream Plants presents a collection of plants in photo essays and plantings and classifies them into combinations that have been in existence since the eighties. These formed the basis of Piet Oudolf's matrix planting: in this approach, the garden is much more organized, with a selection of perennials as "robust as shrubs" that keep each other in check. The initial diversity, the never-ending variation of grasses, plants, flower-filled thickets resembling millefleur tapestries quickly transformed into a kind of guide for good plants. Some became hallmarks: deep red *Astrantia*, *Monarda*, *Cimicifuga*, thistle-like *Eryngium*, and *Gillena trifoliata* are but a few.

But still, it is the debate about natural gardening that inspires its followers. Piet Oudolf designed the High Line plantings, the elevated rail line that passes through parts of Manhattan and along which all kinds of plants have established themselves, a wildly romantic interlude that is a source of fascination to many city dwellers. Advised by German Cassian Schmidt, who collects data in Hermannshof in Weinheim about the lifespan and amount of care required by certain plant combinations, Piet Oudolf designed a tamed wilderness. He also planted the atrium in Peter Zumthor's Serpentine Pavilion in London in 2011 and designed a perennial meadow for the gallery Hauser & Wirth in Somerset, England, for which his design sketches—"a patchwork of colours and symbols"—have become part of an exhibit. Because the meadow was to be spectacular and long-lasting, he expressly used plants that don't compete with one another, don't self-seed, and don't die after flowering: "The meadow isn't wild, it's all in groups, like you see on the drawing."[7]

Another highlight of his work was designing Lurie Garden in Chicago's Millennium Park. A prairie-inspired landscape planted exclusively with perennials and located on the roof of a giant parking garage, the garden is lush, colourful, attractive, and highly decorative against the backdrop of skyscrapers. The *New York Times* praises Oudolf as "the Dutch Prince of a new, highly artistic style of planting."[8]

The Meadow Is Not Wild

Spectacular, artistic, the only thing missing is decorative: the words to describe Piet Oudolf's gardens are revealing. They are the exact words used as biting criticism against the rose-dahlia-and-gladioli gardens of the 1980s. Instead, the gardener-philosophers wanted to focus on a fluid approach to gardening, one that used natural plants and aligned with natural processes, with all their gradients and nuances.

Even though the High Line is now visited by approximately five million people annually, it is still subject to criticism. On the one hand, the gardens highlight the effects of the ornamental border of grasses and plants on their surroundings: a hyper-gentrification that drives away what once existed. Critics describe the feelings of being in a crowd that's corralled from the beginning to the end of the path as similar to those one experiences in an airport's passport queue. And some note that this carefully planted, artificially irrigated version of nature, visited by millions, is nothing but a facsimile when compared to the wild beauty that existed when everything was left to itself, making it "a fairly stifling, uncreative experience."[9]

The Lurie Garden in Chicago's Millennium Park is different. Oudolf was highly praised for his selection of plants (many of which are native to the state of Illinois) and the visible progression of the seasons: plants and grasses wither, colours change, leaf structure becomes important. The project is scientifically supported, and yet here, too, cost-effectiveness is key: there are no annuals, no plants that make the garden haphazard. Instead, it consists of large groupings of the same plant: troops of echinacea, masses of non-fussy salvia varieties. Seen in this way, Piet Oudolf's matrix of select prairie or steppe or other meadow-like plants differentiates itself less and less from the nineteenth-century planting patterns designed for carpet bedding—the exact opposite of what this garden movement once wanted.

Delivering Nature

Nature is not a picture, it's a process. This elevates gardening above landscape painting—it's about practical experience versus purely observing. You have to live a philosophy of gardening. It can only grow through practical action, just as Romke van de Kaa does with his meadow: again and again and again and again, constantly amazed and inquiring, observing the nuances Rob Leopold conjured up and lauded and for which he provided the ingredients, and, thereby creating what was essentially an instruction guide and theory: the plants in his *Dikke Zadenlijst*.

Piet Oudolf, on the other hand, has transformed the natural garden into a product he can deliver, with plant combinations that are guaranteed to work. He refines and improves them according to visual criteria, so they do justice to their assigned task of providing nature. But using the word *nature* alone is not enough. You cannot plug experiencing nature into a formula; the principle of practising being close to nature has to be taken seriously.

The Gardener Fights Back

In the last years of his life, Rob Leopold was increasingly filled with doubt. For example, when he had to supply seeds from his *Dikke Zadenlijst* to turn garbage depots in Amsterdam green: wildflowers to decorate environmental sins? Even his existence as an exuberant faun surrounded by nature was destabilized when the city of Groningen planned a bypass near his home, and heavy machinery started to dig up the soil. In his own way, Rob Leopold fought back, with a gardener's means: he purchased pasture land to use as a buffer zone and once again picked up his shovel, made the soil arable, and sowed flowers.

Elke von Radziewsky studied German and art history, works as an editor and author, and, together with her husband, keeps a big garden. She pursues her interest in garden theory by personally speaking to as many of the most intriguing gardeners and landscape architects as possible in order to understand what they do, and to find out what should be seen.

1   The narrative passages, with original quotes from Rob Leopold and
     Romke van de Kaa, were taken from the following articles: Elke von
     Radziewsky, "Rob Leopold, Gärtner und Guru" [Rob Leopold, Gar-
     dener and Guru], in A&W Architektur & Wohnen 02 (00) (Hamburg:
     Jahreszeiten Verlag GmbH, 2000), and Elke von Radziewsky, "Romke
     van de Kaa, Das Glück ist ein Grasfeld" [Romke van de Kaa, Happiness
     Is a Field of Grass], in A&W Architektur & Wohnen 03 (13) (Hamburg:
     Jahreszeiten Verlag GmbH, 2013).

2   Otto Valentien in Garten und Landschaft [Garden and Countryside]
     (Munich: Georg Verwaltungs GmbH & Co. KG, March 1962), 74–75.

3   Beth Chatto, The Dry Garden (Madison: Dent, 1978); Beth Chatto,
     The Damp Garden (Madison: Dent, 1982); Beth Chatto, Beth Chatto's
     Gravel Garden: Drought-Resistant Planting Throughout the Year (New
     York: Viking Studio, 2000).

4   Richard Hansen, Friedrich Stahl, Perennials and Their Garden Habi-
     tats, trans. Richard Ward (Michigan: Timber Press, 1993).

5   Piet Oudolf, Henk Gerritsen, Dream Plants for the Natural Garden
     (Portland: Timber Press, 2000).

6   Henk Gerritsen, GartenManifest [Garden Manifesto] (Stuttgart: Eugen
     Ulmer Verlag, 2014).

7   "Blueprint" in: "Design Curial" (London: November 13, 2014).

8   Dominique Browning, "Hummelo, a Journey Through A Plantman's
     Life," in New York Times (New York, May 29, 2015).

9   Roland High, "Talk Examines Negative Repercussions of New York's
     High Line Project," in The Brown Daily Herald (Providence: The Daily
     Brown Herald Inc.: September 30, 2015).

DIETER WANDSCHNEIDER

On the Metaphysics of the Garden[1]

1. Introduction

Metaphysics is the philosophical contemplation of fundamental questions regarding earthly and divine existence. Referring to metaphysics, as we do here, might appear somewhat overstated in reference to something as mundane as a garden. The truly big themes of philosophy, according to Kant, are concerned with questions about humanity: What can I know? What should I do? What can I hope for? What is a human being? The question addressed here—namely, "What is a garden?"—is not among them.

Undoubtedly there are philosophical problems more pressing than this, ones that affect our existence and our world. By comparison, a philosophy of the garden seems less urgent. But its charm might just be in taking the opportunity to ignore the seriousness of life and allowing oneself to ask "frivolous" questions, which of course, as we will find out, inadvertently touch upon fundamental questions regarding our existence—questions that typically emerge in the "garden of philosophy."

"The philosophy of the garden" or "the garden of philosophy": even reversed, the phrase makes sense. After all, gardens and parks have always been places of philosophical contemplation. Prominent historic examples of gardens as sanctuaries for *symphilosophizing*—that is, collaborative philosophizing—include Plato's Academy in the grove belonging to the Greek hero Akademos, Aristotle's Peripatos, the famous Lyceum, and Epicurus's philosophy garden Kepos—places in the Athenian landscape where much time was spent discussing the thoughts that would define present-day Europe in terms of intellectual history up to the present day. Even today, beautiful gardens and park-like environments are a favourite place to hold philosophy classes and symposiums—for example, Capri, Ravello on the Amalfi coast, the Académie du Midi in Southern France, or the Rockefeller Foundation's Bellagio Center on the Lake Como peninsula. But why are gardens places of contemplation?

2. Nature and Design

Essentially, the garden exists in the tension between nature and design. It is not simply nature in the sense of wilderness, which exists on its own. But even cultivated natural forms—fields, meadows, forests, etc.—are not gardens, because they lack artistic design. Design is therefore a constitutive element of a garden. But just as importantly, a garden is nature, and therefore subject to conditions of organic growth. This interplay between nature and design forms the central perspective in the present context.

The desired design ideal has always been the beautiful garden. In an inspiring written contribution to the 2012 *Bamberger Hegelwoche*,[2] Christian Illies asks why garden design didn't follow in the footsteps of modern art and transition to ugliness. Even now, gardens and parks are not designed as junkyards or visual provocations, but continue to reflect the traditional ideal of beauty—which, of course, is considered harmonistic and therefore obsolete in modern art and art philosophy.[3]

Illies's statement that garden design is closely linked with the traditional ideal of beauty is certainly true, as are the possible reasons cited for this—the evolutionary nature of people, the use of the garden for recreational purposes, the autonomy of the organic, the fashion-resistant endurance of gardens, our emotional relationship to them. Interestingly, however, these viewpoints have nothing to do with the concept of beauty that Kant's aesthetic canonized, according to which the beautiful elicits indifferent delight in us. The reasons given are pragmatic in nature—that is, guided by interest; the second reason, according to which the garden should "offer people rest and relation, make it possible to experience nature and beautiful impressions,"[4] explicitly relates the garden's effects with being pleasant, which, according to Kant, is *not* beautiful. Well, as a gardening aesthete you may not have to be a Kantian. Still, one question remains unanswered, and I'd like to return to it later.

With respect to the aforementioned tension between nature and design, on the one hand, the natural aspect of the garden is essential; it is the autonomous, primal force of the living. But on the other hand, the garden is also designed nature, art. This raises the fundamental question of what design adds to nature. What does the garden have more of as compared to nature at its most wild and pristine? Is it the garden's beauty? And if so, in the sense of what is known as natural beauty, or the sense of its opposite, namely artistic beauty? The classical aesthetic has repeatedly undertaken divisive discussions on both forms of beauty, at times giving preference to one, at times to the other.

With respect to garden art, this question gives cause for a certain degree of embarrassment. Because the garden is, as stated earlier, both nature and art. On the one hand, its beauty lies in its flowers, ornamental shrubs, and trees. On the other hand, the design is eminently important, because without it, we wouldn't have a garden, but rather, a natural landscape. Both nature and art, that much is certain, enjoy a reciprocal relationship.[5] The creative arrangement sets the stage for nature's performance. In the wild, roses bloom and wither—this is simply a natural process. The garden, on the other hand, is a presentation and celebration of beauty. Only in this way can nature appear in its true form.

Does art have anything to do with the appearance of truth? This brings to mind, for example, Heidegger's interpretation of the Greek temple: "Standing there, the building rests upon the rocky ground. In this resting-upon, the work takes from out of the rock the darkness of its support, unwieldy and yet forced-to-nothing [...] The secure towering-up of the temple makes visible the invisible space of air."[6] "Art does not reproduce the visible; rather, it makes visible," wrote Paul Klee.[7] Indeed, it is through the creative design of the temple that the structure of the rock first appears in relief, just as the expanse of the sky above it serves as its counterpart. Design allows nature to be nature, allows it to appear in its truth. But what is the "truth" of nature? In the designing of a garden, the blossoming of a rose is, as I've stated, more than just a natural process. Here, it is beautiful. Its potential is manifested in the garden: its truth as a rose, which is its beauty.

Plato linked beauty with truth and goodness.[8] A good rose is therefore a beautiful rose. According to this, beauty is that which is good, that which is entirely free of flaws. As such, however, it actually has no place in the real world, but rather, according to Plato, exists as an ideal and for this reason is only understandable intellectually. The fact that this ideal is continuously perceived by the senses—as in the form of a beautiful rose—does not run counter to this: the rose is beautiful when we contemplate it, that is, from an intellectual perspective. The rose itself is only beautiful, but it is unaware of this fact; it is unable to recognize the idea that it embodies.

That beauty possesses an idealistic way of being does not, however, mean that it requires conceptual or logical acknowledgement. It is simply pleasing. As we know, Kant attributes aesthetic judgement to a "state of mind," which stems from "free play of imagination and understanding," which means that, to a certain extent, imagination assists understanding. This "free play of the faculties of imagination and understanding" is punctuated by "pleasure."[9]

Following in the footsteps of Kant, Hegel undertook to recapture the concept of beauty within the context of his conception of idealism. If, in the case of Kant, beauty is determined based on a "state of mind"—that is, subjectively—in the case of Hegel, it is determined ontologically: that is, with respect to its way of being. Hegel's well-known dictum that beauty is "the sensual semblance of the idea" emphasizes—to the extent that it ties in with Plato—its ideal character.[10] Yet Hegel speaks of *the idea*, *idea* in singular, not of *ideas* in plural, like Plato. This understanding of *idea* represents the divine, which, particularly in the sensory context of the reality of nature, appears as beauty—a notion that has already been hinted at above, but whose metaphysical content remains to be clarified.

3. The Atmospheric

I shall begin with one of Gernot Böhme's fundamental criticisms of the classic concept of beauty, according to which the essential aesthetic theories of the sensory are mostly excluded, as they are too "cerebral." What is missing is an "ecologically motivated aesthetic" that essentially also integrates "emotional components," that is, "states of feeling," which Böhme, in response to Hermann Schmitz, calls "atmospheres" and characterizes as forms of "physical and sensory experience."[11] The physical-sensory person and their "state of mind" is, according to Böhme, "the appropriate bioindicator."[12]

It makes perfect sense that observations like this are also relevant to an *aesthetic of the garden*. With regard to a more pragmatic "Theory of Landscape Gardening," Böhme notes that it has already "dealt with the topic of" "that which was frowned upon in otherwise middle-class aesthetics, namely, that which 'goes to the heart'":[13] beauty "as a type of nourishment,"[14] "namely sensuous-emotional,"[15] so, something like "food for the soul." The beauty of a garden's environment is the magical effect of nature's living presence on both the senses and the emotions: the cozy, the intellectually stimulating, comforting, inspirational, contemplative, worthy, solemnity of a place such as this. For human beings, who also have a sensuous existence, "one of the fundamental needs of life [...] is not just the desire for a beautiful environment in general, [...] but especially the need for nature: namely, something that is there of its own accord, and which touches you through its automatic presence."[16] In fact, gardens and parks cannot be emotionally replaced by artificial environments. One might enjoy the hustle and bustle and the clever contrivances of an amusement park, but it cannot replace nature. But why? An explanation is still pending.

This psychological need for nature, which is also expressed in the design of gardens, is clearly something that is characteristic of humans. Animals do not have gardens, even if, as physical and emotional beings, it's undoubtedly true that nature also does them good. I think that, in this regard, for people an emotional surplus is observed, which cannot be chalked up to "nature does good." So, once again: the coziness, the intellectually stimulating, comforting, inspirational, contemplative, dignified, solemnity of a garden environment is nothing that couldn't be attributed more meaningfully and realistically to the experience of animals. Higher-order animals certainly have emotions, but do not appreciate gardens, which is why they don't create any.

What conclusions can we draw from this? I would like to sum it up as follows: garden culture is a matter of specifically human and, as such, intellectual achievements. Even the "horticultural sense" of the atmospheres in gardens and parks is essentially intellectual in nature. This is the hypothesis that I would like to delve into in more detail, further to the grandiose philosophical proposal put forth by Hegel, which is now increasingly coming into focus.

4. Hegel's Concept of Nature and Consequences for the Relationship to Nature

My hypothesis, that the "horticultural sense" is significantly conceptual in nature, is based on Hegel's notion that nature itself is grounded in the ideal and can only be intellectually grasped as such. To indicate clearly that this is not merely a philosophical affirmation, I would like to outline at least a little of the argument on which Hegel's philosophy of objective idealism is based.

The attribute "objective" indicates that Hegel's philosophy is based on the objective reliability of logic—not on a formal logic, but rather on the fundamental logic on which it is based. This forms the basis of the Hegelian proposal, his ultimate foundation. Its ultimate justification, as we would say now, is based on the fact that this cannot be justified on the basis of an extra-logical instance, because justification itself is a logical act; it already implies logic. Fundamental logic is thus understood as inevitably absolute. This is easily tested: those who attempt to circumvent logic by doubting it are already implying logic, because even the act of doubting is a logical one. There is no way to—"absolutely"—get around logic: the well-known argument of self-alienation from skepticism.

The absolutism of logic, or, in Hegel's parlance, the "idea," is now, according to Hegel, also the reason for the existence of nature. Thus, it has not just logical but also ontological significance: it is based in the absolute idea—that is, the ideal— understood as fundamental logic. The absolutism of the ideal means that it is unconditional, and that means it's ultimately independent of the non-ideal—which, in this sense, is always dialectically connected with the ideal. Qua absolutism the non-ideal also always belongs to the ideal: nature! But as the non-ideal, nature nonetheless continues to be based on the ideal, and determined by it. This is expressed through the law of nature. According to this, to put it very briefly, nature as the non-ideal is established in the logical ideal: as it were, as a logically necessary, eternal accompanying phenomenon of the logical ideal.[17]

So, nature grounded in the ideal? In our current metaphysics-averse era, this might seem strange. Yet this notion is supported by important natural scientists, including Max Born,[18] Albert Einstein,[19] Werner Heisenberg,[20] Carl Friedrich von Weizsäcker, to name a few;[21] because are natural laws not actually akin to the logic that underlies nature? Actual nature is grounded in a logical ideal—in the context of this illustrated argument (but only here), I feel this to be irrefutable.

Now the question is: what are the implications for our relationship with nature? First, we need to understand that nature is made up of more than clay or dirt. The consequence of its intrinsic law is that its being does not give rise to its respective limited factuality, but rather contains substantial ability, such as the ability to create complex systems, to create systems in which organisms evolve, to create psychological and, last but not least, intellectual effort. Nature includes these possibilities qua the laws of nature, thanks to their logically ideal reasons. But the logically ideal is the absolute, the divine, in which nature participates. That nature "is there of its own accord," is self-producing, is therefore creational in nature, *natura naturans*, is actually explicable through its manifestation of the divine.

From an objective-idealist perspective, nature is thus to be interpreted as a manifestation of its underlying ideal principle, as an "image of divine reason," as Hegel states.[22] In other words: in the form of a self-perpetuating, continuously rebirthing *natura naturans*, and only thus, humans have a direct view of an eternally existing divine and, consequently, an essential interest in preserving a living, intact, constantly flourishing nature.

With this, I feel I've opened up a perspective that also sheds light on our topic of the garden. The garden, so to speak, is the temple that preserves nature. Yes, fundamentally, "everything that is supposed to flourish," according to Heinrich Rombach, needs the "structure of a garden." Figuratively speaking, this could also apply to the flourishing of a family, society, the state—and understood in this way, through Rombach, we could literally talk about a "right to a garden."[23]

5. The Metaphysics of the Garden

I've already explained that the garden, as structured nature, always contains an intellectual moment—as stated above: animals do not have gardens. But what appeals to us in gardens and parks, what moves us, or perhaps enchants us—the peculiar atmosphere of the garden—is definitely not simply the symmetry of shapes in the French version, or the interplay of landscape scenes in an English park, or the composition of colourful flowerbeds. It is certain that in designs such as this, the designing spirit encounters itself, but what is special about them is the empathetically perceived life force of nature, which moves us.

But it is also not simply nature, because this would give us the impression of arbitrary proliferation, of wilderness, or of wasteland and barrenness. Sure, there are also situations in which the presence of the great outdoors appeals to us instantly, perhaps when we see a mountain landscape, a lovely meadow, a sandy desert, or a row of poplars along a river—characteristic atmospheric values. This atmospheric element is, admittedly, a very fleeting quality—something that inspires a photographer to take a picture or a landscape artist to paint. Now the image becomes an artifact and, as such, is no longer nature, but rather a representation of nature. Nature makes its appearance through the medium of art and is, as such, denatured. We observe a representation of nature, but we are not embedded in it.

You can probably guess what I'm getting at: compared to the pictorial representation of nature, the garden is the real, sensory presence of nature—and not simply nature, as it is when we occasionally encounter mountain landscapes, wasteland, sandy deserts, poplar-lined roads, but rather nature simultaneously as the enactment of the secret of growth, passing, and re-emergence. Here, the design is significant. Horticultural design brings nature into the sphere of people's lives and presents it as burgeoning, mysterious growth, as continuous rebirth, as vibrant, radiant nature. To portray this, garden art, as opposed to the "beautiful" arts, does not use pigments, sound frequencies, or theatre stages, but rather allows the living to speak to the living.

In this atmosphere of emphatic vitality, if I may express myself thus, I am a part of nature in all its grandeur, its oneness. In this cosmic unanimity, I can momentarily let go of and forget the hunted and the chased, the burden of my finite existence. This is *not* possible within the walls of a house. The cosmic moment is missing within our four walls and cannot be found in the hostile context of the streets. In a garden, we experience a cosmic unanimity with nature, and it does us good.

So then: "Nature does us good." Yes, of course, but *why*? Because, and here I embrace what is clear from the perspective of the Hegelian concept of nature: in the end, this feeling of cosmic unanimity points beyond nature, to something that lies at its very root, its raison d'être and the reason for all being. What occurs to me is that I myself am not the ultimate ground, but rather, I am linked to an ontological principle that underlies me and nature in equal measure, a final ground and, in this sense, something divine.

Therefore, a metaphysics of the garden! Again: is this too overstated? I maintain that the Hegelian argument that *logic* underlies not just the intellect, but also, implicitly, nature, is irrefutable—logic, which we encounter as the laws of nature. We can identify these laws—that is, logically spell them out. But we can also, as it were, "horticulturally" experience them. Think of the beauty of a rose, with its delicate, silken petals and colours, which are a marvel in contrast to the dull soil from which it grows—Rilke's "Rose, oh pure contradiction." In fact, the rose reveals a secret to the intellect: namely, that the earth always contains the ability to flower; this is its hidden reality. Remember: beauty is the appearance of truth. This is evidence that the earth is, in truth, more than shapeless dirt; it is the ideal principle underlying nature, which is also the principle of the intellect.[24] That's why, as intellectual beings, we not only feel ourselves respond to the peacefulness produced by a garden and the landscape architect's compositional design, but, on a much deeper level, to the apparent reality of living, vibrant nature. Are we not always looking for such places to replenish our strength? How does this strength grow? Because nature figuratively provides us with a view of our own essence. The intellect and nature thereby reveal—in spite of all their differences—an essential affinity that grants us a deep sense of oneness in which we take part. This underground cosmic union of intellect and nature, the divine, is what constitutes the magic of spending quiet time in a garden.

I feel that it is also clear that this divine is not to be imagined as being situated in the *other world*. The *metaphysical* is defined literally as that which goes beyond nature, but in this case is certainly not in an otherworldly sense, but rather as a delving into the *ground* of nature, which, from a Hegelian perspective, is also the ground of the intellect. The happy choice of the term *atmospheric* seems to me to actually mean this inner awareness of cosmic harmony, the union of intellect and nature—and thus so much more than the above-quoted "experience of the independent activity of nature," with people in the role of a bioindicator.

But at the same time—and here I return to the earlier question, which still remains unanswered—this cosmic harmony also cannot be reduced to that which is pleasant about an environment and provides respite; that is, the merely pleasant, which Kant had—rightly so, in my opinion—countered with the beautiful. The atmosphere that surrounds us in gardens and in parks satisfies us, enchants us, intellectually draws our attention instead to that which is more than mere nature, but that is always present within it as its imminent truth: the divine as the essential unity of intellect and nature.

When I look out the window, what do I see? Weeds are taking over, it's time to mow the lawn, to get the aphids under control, trim the hedges, level out the mole hills. The gaps between the patio slabs are grown over with moss. There is much to do. But there's also that back pain. The very prosaic pragmatism of garden work! "*Metaphysics* of the garden!?" Certainly—why else would we take on all that?

Dr. Dieter Wandschneider: 1983–87 Professor of Philosophy (Tübingen), 1988–2004 Chair of Philosophy and Scientific Theory at the RWTH Aachen University. Publications primarily in the fields of natural philosophy, the philosophy of logic, particularly dialectic logic, Hegel interpretations, the philosophy of technology, and the mind-body problem.

1 The text is based on a talk I gave on June 13, 2012, for the 2012 Bamberger Hegelwoche.

2 TN: An annual, week-long event hosted by the University of Bamberg to which great minds from the fields of science, politics, and art are invited to hold talks.

3 Dieter Wandschneider, "Das Geistige und das Sinnliche in der Kunst—Hegel, Heidegger, Adorn" [The Spiritual and the Sensual in Art—Hegel, Heidegger, Adorn] in Dieter Wandschneider (Ed.), Das Geistige und das Sinnliche in der Kunst. Ästhetische Reflexion in der Perspektive des Deutschen Idealismus [The Spiritual and the Sensual in Art. Aesthetic Reflections on the Perspectives of German Idealism] (Würzburg: Königshausen & Neumann, 2005).

4 Christian Illies, "Das hässliche Gärtlein? Über die Beharrlichkeit des Schönen in der Gartenkunst" [The Ugly Little Garden? On the Endurance of the Beautiful in Garden Art] in uni.vers. Das Magazin der Otto-Friedrich-Universität Bamberg. Forschung Mai 2012 [uni.vers. The OttoFriedrich-University of Bamberg magazine] (Bamberg: Haßfurter MEDIENPARTNER GmbH & Co. KG, 2012).

5 Christian Hirschfeld, Theory of Garden Art, trans. Linda B. Parshall (taken from an abridged version with an epilogue written by Franz Ehmke) (Berlin: Union Verlag, 1990), 157.

6 Martin Heidegger, The Origin of the Work of Art, trans. Albert Hofstadter (New York: Harper and Row, 1977).

7 Paul Klee, Creative Confession, translation copyright Thames & Hudson (Millbank: Tate Publishing, 2013).

8 For example, Politeia 517 b, c; Timaios 29a, e. (Plato—quoted according to Stephanus pagination).

9 Immanuel Kant, Critique of the Power of Judgement (Kritik der Urteilskraft, 1790), trans. Paul Guyer and Eric Matthews (Cambridge: Cambridge University Press, 2000).

10 Georg Wilhelm Friedrich Hegel, Werke in 20 Bänden [Works in 20 volumes], ed. Eva Moldenhauer and Karl Markus Michel (Frankfurt a. M.: Suhrkamp, 1969).

11 Gernot Böhme, Für eine ökologische Naturästhetik [Toward an Ecological Aesthetics of Nature] (Frankfurt a. M.: Suhrkamp, 1989), 11 et seq.

12 Ibid., 50.

13 Ibid., 46 and 93.

14 Ibid., 47.

15 Ibid., 93.

16 Ibid., 92.

17 For greater detail, see Dieter Wandschneider, "Die Absolutheit des Logischen und das Sein der Natur. Systematische Überlegungen zum absolut-idealistischen Ansatz Hegels" [The Absolutism of the Logical and the Existence of Nature. Systematic Considerations on Hegel's Absolute-Idealistic Approach], in Zeitschrift für philosophische Forschung 39 (Frankfurt a. M.: Vittorio Klostermann GmbH, 1985), 331–51.

18 Max Born, Physics in My Generation (New York: Springer, 1969), 114, 160 et seq.

19 Albert Einstein, The World as I See It, trans. Alan Harris (New York: Philosophical Library, Inc., 2010).

20 Werner Heisenberg, Wandlungen in den Grundlagen der Naturwissenschaft [Transformations in the Principles of Natural Science] (Stuttgart: Hirzel, 1980).

21 Carl Friedrich von Weizsäcker, The Unity of Nature, trans. Francis J. Zucker (New York: Farrar Straus Giroux, 1980).

22 Georg Wilhelm Friedrich Hegel, 20.455.

23 Heinrich Rombach. 2011. "Im Garten. Anregungen zu einem hortensischen Lebensmodus" [In the Garden. Inspirations for a Horticultural Way of Life], in Salzkorn (246) (Reichelsheim: Offensive Junger Christen - OJC e.V., 2011).

24 Dieter Wandschneider, "Beauty in Nature Both in Its Laws and Its Entities," in The Many Faces of Beauty, ed. Vittorio Hösle (Indiana: University of Notre Dame Press, 2013), 113–32.

JUDITH HENNING

Urban Permaculture—City Gardening with a Hidden Agenda[1]

> "Though the problems of the world are increasingly complex, the solutions remain embarrassingly simple."—Bill Mollison

> "All the world's problems can be solved in a garden."
> —Geoff Lawton

A permaculture garden is a kitchen garden made up mostly of perennial plants that are beneficial to one another and are often also combined with livestock. The underlying idea behind permaculture rests on an ethical foundation: *Earth Care, People Care, Fair Share*. These are the words of Bill Mollison and David Holmgren, the founders of permaculture.[2] Care for the earth, care for the people, and share fairly.

What do these principles have to do with gardening—how can we solve the world's problems by gardening? And above all, how should this philosophy, developed for rural areas, work in cities?

Large areas of cities are grey and covered in asphalt—dirty and full of buildings, streets, railroads, and subway tunnels. But there are also front gardens and backyards, parks and playgrounds, and in between there are green areas with wonderfully administrative names like *forested buffer zone* or *roadside greenscape*. Even the roofs and walls of buildings can be used.

All combined, there are huge areas that are already planted, or that can be planted. This can even extend to planting *in* buildings, with indoor composting, mushroom cultivation, or window farms.[3] And if you look closely, you can already see the movement growing. Plants are reclaiming empty spaces and grow in the tiniest of cracks, even on buildings. Urban permaculture is trying to work together with this spontaneous vegetation, creating new spaces for it and supplementing it with useful plants. The goal is to identify and take advantage of the many opportunities, materials, and specific environmental conditions in cities to transform barren or paved surfaces into growing spaces and harvesting opportunities, to meet the basic needs of people and other living beings, and to fulfill permaculture's three guiding principles. The following examples show how this can be done.

Asphalt, Roadsides, and Courtyards

San Francisco's Hayes Valley Farm has transformed a former freeway on-ramp into an urban farm. There are raised beds with vegetables, fruit trees in mortar tubs and a stream bed lined with repurposed broken pieces of concrete (called urbanite) that distributes rainwater throughout the property. This is all growing on top of asphalt covered in cardboard, wood chips, and compost—materials delivered by the city's waste management service. Composted kitchen waste was added once a week, arriving in five wheelbarrows delivered by a commercial kitchen from a nearby Buddhist centre. Layers upon layers of organic waste and recycled paper transformed a street in the heart of the city into a vegetable-producing refuge, which soon became home to a multitude of wild birds, in addition to the urban farmers' bees and chickens.

In the middle of London, in an industrial district near King's Cross station, Alex Smith, the founder of the muesli company Alara, decided to tackle the neglected roadsides.

The narrow strips of land around his production plant were transformed into an incredible garden. There is a tiny vineyard, a fruit tree orchard, and a communal garden. A roadside shoulder has been planted with an unbelievably diverse array of fruit trees, shrubs, and edible perennials. Trees known to sequester nitrogen serve as fertilizer while also providing berries; the hedge also acts as a plantation that will provide wood in a few years for future fence posts. Everything is watered using rainwater from a nearby rooftop, which is distributed over the slightly sloping terrain with the help of gravity.

Let's look at Berlin's Café Botanico, which goes one step further. The permaculture garden in the courtyard behind the café, which also consists mostly of perennial plants, provides the salad greens served in the café. The principle: whatever happens to be ripe is put on the menu. The garden also houses several beehives, and honey from the hives is sold in the café. Through direct marketing (and minimal food transportation), the cafe's compost cycle is a closed loop, and the economics are also highly efficient—a peculiarity that works even better in the city, because of population density, than it would in the country.[4]

These examples show a few of the design principles underlying urban permaculture gardens: beneficial connections are made within the garden, and from the garden outward; attempts are made to achieve good yields, and to proceed in an energy-efficient manner, through multi-functionality and the skilful arrangement of elements. The use of resources others see as waste is copied from nature: there is no garbage in ecosystems; everything a living being leaves behind is eaten by others or otherwise used. And instead of selecting high-quality land, neglected or undeveloped areas are often regenerated for these gardens.

Perennials are typical to permaculture, not just for fruit, but also for vegetable gardens. Making use of permanent or recurring plant growth, and taking advantage of the overwintering capabilities of certain plants, reduces the amount of work. Once established, plants like dock or sorrel (which is used much in the same way as Swiss chard or spinach), which have deep and widely branching roots, are much less sensitive to drought, snails, or aphids than newly seeded vegetables. And they go dormant during the winter, meaning a new garden doesn't have to be prepared in following years.

Like a typical organic garden, permaculture gardens do not use pesticides, chemical fertilizers, or peat. Plant diseases and harmful insects are kept under control through companion planting, crop rotation, and organic biostimulants such as nettle, horsetail, or green manure made with comfrey leaves. Compost is used as a fertilizer. Crop-bearing plants, flowering plants and ponds, and piles of brush or rocks create habitats for beneficial insects, thereby enhancing the ecosystem as a whole.

And in a garden that is designed as an edible landscape, harvesting is part of the maintenance. For example, if I cut back my sage plant, I don't have to deal with getting rid of the cuttings, because I have a bunch of herbs I can enjoy as a healthy and delicious tea, and then add to my compost pile. In choosing an edible plant, I'm using it more intensively, and it becomes something of value, rather than something to be discarded. This principle may seem banal at first glance, but it holds great potential for conserving energy.

However, urban green spaces are not normally designed to be either particularly natural or utilitarian; instead, the emphasis in public spaces is that they be perpetually green and as low-maintenance as possible. In private areas, design often follows the long-established template of lawn, roses, and conifers (the latter is increasingly being replaced by cherry laurel). From a permaculture perspective, these spaces are like green deserts—so, the exact opposite of what permaculture aspires to. Harvest? Non-existent! Lawns need to be mowed, maintained, and fertilized, which means investing a lot of time and energy for purely decorative purposes.

Permaculture uses a different approach: green spaces are no longer seen as annoying, potentially messy-looking strips that require maintenance and cost money. Instead, any green space, or even any available space, including walls and roofs, is seen for its potential harvest. When considered from this perspective, the city can be viewed in a different light: glass-covered office facades—wonderful greenhouses; round-abouts—a flower meadow; the protected south-facing wall of a high-rise—a vineyard? Suddenly, the city is overflowing with planting opportunities, perhaps the most compelling of which are rooftops.

Roofs and Balconies

Provided they are protected from the wind, rooftops provide ideal growing conditions—they tend to be sunny, and in cities, the microclimate is often milder because the stone-covered surfaces store heat. In addition, building technology provides the potential for useful combinations: the warm exhaust from cooling units can be used to heat greenhouses, while the condensation from air conditioning systems can be used for irrigation. The building thus becomes a resource for the garden growing on it.

A research team from the University of Bologna sees, for example, a great deal of potential for rooftop gardens: it posits that if every suitable roof surface in Bologna were used, 77 percent of the city's vegetable needs could be met by cultivation in their own city. In addition, 624 tonnes of CO_2 per year would be captured, and further energy savings would result from reduced transport distances. And provided the rooftop gardens were farmed using environmentally friendly principles, they would also create their own ecosystem.[5]

The current ideas are not limited to vegetables alone: a Berlin company is selling aquaponic systems and has set up a rooftop demo farm in Schöneberg to show how successful it is. The system cultivates tomatoes, lettuce, and fish. The water from the fish tank is used to water the plants, and the fish waste provides fertilizer.

A rooftop farm that was planned into the construction of a hospital in Singapore incorporates additional utilitarian aspects: in a tropical climate, the plants (in addition to providing patients with fresh vegetables) have a considerable cooling effect on the building, thereby reducing energy costs related to air conditioning. Furthermore, the rooftop garden becomes a soothing and therapeutic oasis in a densely populated island and city state.[6]

But this can also be done on a much smaller scale at home. I cultivate fruits and vegetables on my balcony, which is actually no more than a thirty-centimetre-wide windowsill with a railing. It has a total surface area of one square metre—I grow fruits and vegetables on a small scale. I have a shrubby blackberry growing in an old garbage pail; beside it is a zucchini plant in a bag of potting soil, and I've turned a reinforced flowerpot into a potato tower. There are also vine tomatoes, Hokkaido pumpkins, and I've planted salad greens, Swiss chard, kale, some herbs, and edible flowering plants like borage and nasturtiums in window boxes and flowerpots. The soil consists of worm compost made with my household vegetable waste, mixed with leached potting soil.

Once things started flowering, bumblebees, hoverflies, and other bees appeared, and this summer, a blackbird even sought refuge under the zucchini leaves, where she built a nest and raised her brood. I harvested 2.5 kilograms of zucchini, between one and two kilograms of tomatoes, two pumpkins, five hundred grams of blackberries, and herbs, potatoes, Swiss chard, and salad greens—all in the first year. Even a tiny balcony can become an oasis that not only provides animals with a habitat and food, but also an impressive harvest for such a small area.

This demonstrates the diversity and abundance that is possible in a small space, and how quickly interdependence can be established with the surrounding ecosystem. However, the rest of the house's facade consists only of stone and glass. If every balcony were to be similarly greenscaped, it would be like paradise. In keeping with permaculture principles, balconies could be automatically watered using the downspouts. Each apartment's rent could include one espalier fruit tree, plus a few bags of soil. And there could also be a composting system in the basement to deal with the building's green waste—a bit unusual, but not all that complicated to implement.

In addition to good soil, water is a key element for ensuring a successful container garden. Those who can't access rainwater can find other solutions, like waste-water from washing vegetables or rinsing out the coffee machine, as long as it contains no salt or detergents. Strictly speaking, most kitchen grey water is ideal for watering plants. Now I collect this water in a bowl and use it for my watering. If the water contains a few crumbs, coffee grinds, or tea leaves, even better, because they also act as fertilizer.

This way, the water, which has already been sanitized via a waste-water purification plant and pumped through pipes to the seventh floor, doesn't simply flow back to the purification plant through the pipes; instead, it remains in my balcony garden. There, it allows edible plants to grow and is evaporated through their leaves, which improves the air and creates a microclimate that is less dry. The grey water from the kitchen thus becomes part of the gardening process on the balcony. Instead of the water being removed as waste, and then filling a watering can with fresh water specifically pumped into your home for the plants, these two processes are integrated and connected such that the waste from one becomes the nourishment for another.

Obviously, a balcony garden cannot serve as your sole food source, but being able to take things into your own hands by creating a cycle—in which you use the soil from your worm composter to pot your plants and then harvest the food you've grown—is a valuable experience. On the one hand, these skills can be applied to larger areas, and on the other hand, growing your own food on a smaller scale is a wonderful experience. The word *culture* stems from *cultura*—growing, cultivation. We are thus engaging in the foundation of our civilization and, to a certain extent, responding in a radically cultural fashion, if we momentarily put aside the modern-day division of labour and consumption and take up shovels ourselves. If we connect with natural cycles, and act in a networked, integrated way—as trivial and commonplace our own actions might be—it will signify a fundamental disalienation.

More Than "Just Digging Around in the Dirt"

A program in the English town of Todmorden, and Hamburg, Germany's KulturEnergieBunkerAltonaProjekt, are not just about gardening in vacant or newly seized areas, but also about building a community and productively using a city's special features. Both demonstrate how impetus can be successfully generated for an entire community from the bottom up to bring about actual change.

The goal of the Incredible Edible Todmorden initiative is to make the city edible. Ideally, edible plants are to be cultivated in all public green spaces and open areas, and also in as many private gardens as possible. Everything growing in public spaces can be freely harvested by all city inhabitants and visitors. This is about caring for people through equitable sharing, and the project's accomplishments have a tangible effect on community life in Todmorden. Since the start of this citizens' movement, the crime rate in this small city has dropped an incredible 12 percent.[7]

This initiative has resonated worldwide, and there are a few edible cities in Germany. One of the most prominent examples is Andernach, where part of the green area near former city fortifications was converted into a vegetable garden. But even in cities like Heidelberg, Halle, Hanover, and Minden, people are coming together to plant forest gardens, build raised beds, and transform neglected rose borders into vegetable plots.

The key goal of Hamburg's Energy Bunker Project was to convert a World War II high-rise bunker into a thermal power station that recycles wood waste from the surrounding parks into heat. The heat feeds directly into the adjacent district pipeline to supply households in the area, the motto being local heat instead of district, or centralized, heat. The proceeds from the sale of the heat are intended to fund the use of the rest of the bunker as a cultural space. A different basic need is being addressed here, and the urban green space becomes an extended garden for the supply of heat. In addition to the long-term goal of urban development from the ground up, a local association put in a community garden near the bunker that consists of raised beds, an outdoor clay oven, a composting toilet, and beehives. In conjunction with regular collective baking and gardening, various other events take place here. The people involved with the association are cultivating a transformation, one in which a society is able to manage on less energy while using local resources.[8] Instead of using a vocabulary of decline and sacrifice, the focus is on growth: not growth based on the usual economic indicators, but rather the growth of community, productive ecosystems, and a local economy.

Looking at Things in Perspective

While these projects are all quite different, they share an underlying philosophy. They strive to create alternatives to current societal developments and to not passively allow environmental degradation and climate change to happen. Instead, they try to implement changes that lead to a healthier, more autonomous, environmentally friendly, and social life in a livable city. And to achieve this, people are taking up rakes and shovels.

Around the world, city populations continue to increase; since 2008, the majority of the world's people have lived in urban areas. That's why it's important to start with cities: they have enormous potential—as can be seen in the small collection of urban permaculture projects shared here—to achieve social equity and sustainability goals, and counteract climate change.

But, independent of scenarios where changes have been imposed due to a lack of resources or climate change, a city optimized for food production and energy self-sufficiency can inspire the planning and development of other livable cities, as exemplified not just by Todmorden. A city in which this type of project is implemented according to ecological principles would be livable, more natural, with less food, packaging material and garbage required to be transported by truck; both vegetable gardens and compost piles would be within walking distance. And there would be more electric vehicles, thereby drastically reducing exhaust and noise pollution. The many small, decentralized production facilities and projects would lead to greater autonomy. Cities would be designed by their citizens, which, in the end, would also lead to more social equity here in Germany, and in other parts of the world over which we have influence. Because it is through these shifts that we can transition from conditions of production designed to serve ignorant consumers back to once again becoming producers of essential goods—or at least come closer to doing so. The examples described here form building blocks, or cycles, that can be implemented in even their most basic forms in city apartments with minimal space, and that could have powerful effects if adopted by many people. This would of course require extensive infrastructure redevelopment—a considerable challenge that could technically be overcome with the necessary political will.

Permaculture has the potential to provide society with a new, expansive, system-wide, and cross-cultural vision. Instead of pitting economic, social, and environmental interests against one another, the goal should be to systematically think them through together and take on the global challenges they pose. Just as the rivalry between the communist and capitalist systems drove nations to land people on the moon, now states, businesses, and other institutions could compete to convert our cultural landscape into efficient and productive ecosystems, and construct modern-day wonders of the world—like hanging gardens in cities.

Judith Henning is a historian, a cobbler, and, in 2012, she also became a permaculture designer. Her focus is on urban permaculture solutions. She divides her time between Hamburg and San Francisco, where she works on small and large gardens, container gardens, vermicomposting, and composting toilets. More recently, she has been planting herbs and vegetables on balconies. In addition to garden-based solutions and resource-related considerations, her projects often involve participative approaches and networking. www.judithhenning.de

1   I would like to thank Frank Wolf and Miriam V. Maydell for their ideas and their help in taming the sheer volume of materials, and Blanka Stolz and Silke Schipper for the inspiration they provided in crucial moments.

2   Bill Mollison, David Holmgren, Permaculture: A Designers' Manual (Tyalgum: Tagari Publications, 1988).

3   For a window farm, herbs, greens, and other small vegetable plants are hung in a window, and the pots are often homemade, using recycled plastic bottles. The plants are usually grown hydroponically—that is, using an inorganic substrate with a nutrient solution—and they benefit from the natural light coming in through the window and the heat provided by the rooms.

4   Judith Henning, "Aus dem Garten auf den Teller. Das Berliner Café Botanico verbindet auf smarte Weise Anbau und Vermarktung" [From the Garden to Plate. The Berlin Café Botanico Intelligently Combines Farming and Marketing] in Oya 27 (Klein Jasedow: Oya Medien eG, July/August 2014), 82–83.

5   Francesco Orsini et al., "Exploring the Production Capacity of Rooftop Gardens (RTGs) in Urban Architecture: The Potential Impact on Food and Nutrition Security, Biodiversity and Other Ecosystem Services in the City of Bologna," in Food Security 6. 781-792. DOI: 10.1007/s12571-014-0389-6.

6   Donal Wai Wing Tai, "Beyond Skyrise Gardens. The Potential of Urban Roof-Top Farming in Singapore," in CTBUH Research Paper (paper presented to the Council of Tall Buildings and Urban Habitat World Conference, Seoul, October 10–12, 2011) (Seoul: CTBUH 2011 Seoul Conference, 2011), 413–427.

7   To read more about the concept, the history, and the current state of the project in Todmorden, in addition to reports on the initiative, see www.incredible-edible-todmorden.co.uk.

8   Very similar ideas and concrete suggestions about how this process of societal transformation can be developed are found in a book written by Rob Hopkins, the founder of the Transition Town movement: Rob Hopkins, The Transition Handbook: From Oil Dependency to Local Resilience (Cambridge: Greenbooks, 2008).

DAGMAR PELGER

Gardening is Commoning

Gardens are, like works of art, rather large fields of experimentation in which each era tentatively advances ideas that they have not yet developed into suitable theories.[1]

On a first visit to Berlin's Prinzessinnengarten, located near high-traffic Moritzplatz, you cannot help but marvel. It's a garden oasis in the middle of the city. Where there was once a fallow vacant lot, it is now a place like those visited on excursions outside the city or on trips home to the countryside, where family members and relatives still cultivate and farm small parcels of land. At the same time, the fenced-in field with its closely spaced container beds seems both foreign and familiar. As a community garden, the Prinzessinnengarten has grown into a veritable institution; it is part of the city's sightseeing and socio-cultural repertoire, is shared on social media from Korea to New York, and yet finds itself regularly threatened by commercial interests. In addition to flower-beds, a library, a beer garden with a summer kitchen, and various other DIY structures, after seven years of gardening, in the summer of 2016, the arbour arrived: a wooden, accessible, three-storey structure intended to serve primarily as an event location for the garden's neighbouring academy (which was founded in 2014), but is open to everyone.

What role do these and the many other urban community gardens that have sprouted up in the last decade play in a resurgent understanding of cities, which are supposed to belong to everyone and give rise to places that attempt to evade market logic and dogmatic austerity? Can possibility be read into this new garden type as a potential place[2] to make urban resources accessible as common goods for a community-based production of urban spaces? The developmental history of the garden as a restricted, structured, exterior space must be viewed alongside the history of common land—unparcelled, collectively cultivated public property. How can the urban community garden be described and understood as it exists at the junction of these two different types of open space?

Gardens are artificially created, scaled-down representations of the natural spaces surrounding a city or village. In them, nature is either reproduced in a condensed version or interpreted in a contrasting manner. Agrarian motifs are borrowed from the landscape, and they are imitated in a painterly, picturesque fashion, or formally stylized. Through their gardening work, whether labour-intensive or nurturing, the gardener feels driven to bring nature to an idealized state. They do this in order to increase the yields of their garden and regenerate their plants, the natural resource. Here, in addition to the material returns—the tomato—immaterial returns—such as its scent—can offer motivation.

The first gardens were primarily kitchen gardens—fenced in to protect them from animals and others interested in their bounty—that produced fruit or herbs. They were followed soon after by flowers and other ornamental plants, which served as sources of enjoyment or as a display of one's gardening talent. The garden can serve as a place for communication and the exchange of ideas, and as a shared place to congregate, overshadowed by the purpose of representation. A garden can also serve to convey knowledge, and as a collection, display, and reproduction facility for various types of plants and animals. In the eclectic gardens of past decades, we find the wildest combinations of garden types, and thus a multitude of overlapping references, design elements, and intentions.

According to Lucius Burckhardt, one thing all gardens have in common is that they represent the current relationship between society and nature.[3] For example, the peasants' kitchen garden recounts the variety of fruit- and flower-bearing plants domesticated by that respective society, and of its dependence on nature for subsistence and survival. The botanical garden was created in the era of expeditions and colonial pilfering, and symbolizes the discoveries made, the appropriation of new goods through nomenclature, and the dissemination of seeds and plants. The geometrical Baroque garden is the representation of nature as controlled by humankind, in stark contrast to the untamed and wild aspect of nature. During the Age of Enlightenment, society was obsessed with a romantic notion of nature, as manifest in English landscape gardens. These gardens portray the ideal of nature as wild and picturesque, intended to charm, inspire, and reward city dwellers, and for this purpose recreates scenes of apparent agricultural use. With the emerging bourgeoisie, gardens and parks increasingly found their way into cities, establishing themselves as city gardens, and later, as garden cities.

Lastly, the modern garden conveys a social image of nature, there to offset the burden of industrialization borne by city dwellers and to promote health and well-being, in addition to providing more affordable food. This garden paints a picture of nature as a well-organized system, one that serves to provide light and clean air to settlements and cities. Nature becomes an infrastructural building block for a new, functionally designed urban landscape in which gardens and parks are used for the purposes of recreation and restoration. Postmodern society, on the other hand, surrenders the transparent, meaningful context between city and country, and thus the structural legibility of its relationship with nature. A collection of images emerges in hybridized gardens, which, as part of the postmodern urban landscape, according to Burckhardt, harmonizes with their "loquacity."[4] Juxtaposed with this actual voicelessness, and in reaction to environmental destruction and nature conservation, a new political movement gives rise to the ecotope garden, as an image of nature that has become increasingly rare.

Burckhardt ends by referring to what is for him the newest and most avant-garde type of garden: the Basler Stadtgärtnerei, which, from 1986 to 1988, was occupied by alternative artists and self-proclaimed Stadtgärtnerinnen und Stadtgärtnern (male and female city gardeners), among others.[5] The garden, which the occupation made accessible to all Basel residents—its dismantling and transformation into a public park could not be prevented, despite widespread popular support—is described by Burckhardt as five overlapping images: the garden as spontaneous vegetation, as rare wilderness, as a farm, as an emergency situation (or crisis), and as utopia.[6] This description of the occupied garden, which can be seen as a forerunner of the contemporary urban community garden, projects the image of a society's politicized relationship with nature. Whereas the peasants' garden highlighted nature's economic role, the Baroque garden represented the absolutist need to rule over nature, the English garden exhibited a romanticized and seemingly economically independent relationship with nature, the modern garden typified nature's social function, and the environmental garden portrayed nature as a rarity threatened by extinction, the urban community garden depicts nature as a political opportunity for society to take a stand on dwindling resources and climate change.

The history of gardens can be compared to another history: common land's role in the formation of jointly owned property. The Allmende, as it is called in Swiss-German, stems from

Middle High German al(ge)meind and refers to a land management system where a spatially defined agricultural area is used by the community; this can be seen as the prototype of the community garden. Established as a concept in the early middle ages, the Allmende—referred to as *commons* in English—denotes the joint ownership of a resource. In the form of a parcel of forest, a meadow, or the right to use a body of water, the traditional commons served to supply its community of users with wood, a pasturing area, fish, or space for cultivation—in other words, as a community kitchen garden in the broadest sense. This area was always unparcelled, usually enclosed, and access was managed by the community.

The rules were independently negotiated among the users—or *commoners*, i.e., those who take care of common land—which was usually tolerated by the feudal owner, though not always. In addition to being attached to a concrete resource, the commons was also characterized by its strong relationship to action: no commons without commoning, according to historian Peter Linebaugh in his studies of the Magna Carta as the first legal protection of the commons.[7] He emphasizes the reproductive nature of the commons, which can only be maintained through constant renewal. This is one of the essential parallels to the definition of a garden.

Building on this definition, philosopher Lieven De Cauter distinguishes between universal and specific common goods with respect to the commons. He counts air or language, which belong to everyone and no one, among the "universal commons" that must be made available to all humans. He designates common goods as "particular commons" that are produced and preserved by a defined community. It can thus be inferred that the commons forms a "heterotopic" or "third" space that can neither be classified as public, state-controlled space, nor as privatized space for individual or co-operative use.[8]

A closer look at four historical types of commons—pasture, hay meadow, grassland, and village green—reveals various locations of common land in the natural resource space. When applied to the contemporary urban landscape, it is possible to draw speculative conclusions about potential new urban commons. The developmental history of traditional commons follows a migration of sorts, from mountains or forests via the open countryside to settlements—in a manner of speaking, from the external to the internal. Seen this way, this developmental sequence can also be portrayed as a type of urbanization of the commons, the continuation of which might be found in modern-day urban commons.

On an early form of commons developed on alpine pastures more than three thousand years ago, the management of annual cycles was usually organized collectively, due to the remote location. Because these pastures were located so far from villages, a need arose early on for seasonal lodging for summer operations, as well as for facilities to process milk. The cycle of pasturing, milk production, and cheese-making to secure food for the winter is still the basis for the significance of the alpine pasture as a seasonal retreat from the city. Its social significance as a place of recreation and memories makes it understandable why the alpine pasture is seen as common property nowadays; they are often still operated co-operatively.

The Hutweide, or hay meadows, were community pastures located on leftover agricultural land closer to a village, which could be used daily or weekly by people and livestock. Situated along the edges of fields, bodies of water, or forests, these areas encouraged the village community to use the land in a specific manner—namely, to tend their cattle. Easily accessible, the hay meadows permitted more regular usage. The Hornbosteler Hutweide, a collectively managed, privately funded pasture land located in Lower Saxony, is a rare example of a revived hay meadow. Through its traditional livestock production methods and small-scale farming, it thereby contributes to the culture of remembrance, knowledge-sharing, and the conservation of the landscape.

As a locally originating, late Middle Ages form of migrating commons, the usage of Vöde, or grasslands, is similar to that of hay meadows. However, because its location changes yearly and is confined to fallow land, the degree to which the village community identifies it as common land is diminished. Up until the middle of the nineteenth century, landless farmers reserved the right to pasture their livestock on the grasslands, but this practice was discontinued with increases in paid labour and industrialization. The former grasslands remained in private hands or were gradually transformed by itinerant field usage into freely accessible, communal property, like the city park in Bochum, Bochumer Stadtpark. Grasslands as loosely structured commons brings to mind current forms of urban provisional use and provides an interesting organizational model based on the principle of land exchange.

The Anger, or village green, located in the village's centre, as the name denotes, was the most urban form of commons. Located in the widened area of the street space, the grassy meadow served as a community vegetable garden or a space for other facilities; the village hall, bake house, smithy, herdsmen's house, or church might be found there. The village residents had a deep-rooted connection to the village green, which served to secure their food supply. As a highly developed leisure area that was incorporated into urban design, the so-called village green was a widespread model in Central and Eastern Europe. For the numerous village greens still in existence, now owned by municipalities as public space, there is no more need for long-standing community conservation practices. But village greens raise questions about resource management in urban spaces. With their central location, spatial serenity, unpaved surfaces, and free access, they become an opportunistic space where the most diverse interests and needs can be dealt with collectively.

The significance and distribution of commons have changed significantly over time. Nowadays, it is rare to see commons as a rural, collectively cultivated property. However, their relocation from the countryside to the village centre has a contemporary sequel in the phenomenon of urban commons. Beginning in the early 1990s, a new discourse has opened up around the commons. The increasing withdrawal of state-run regulatory and supply systems, coupled with increasing competitiveness in many spheres of life, has led to progressive resource scarcity on all levels. The progressive privatization of public goods amplifies demands to include all population levels in economic, political, and planning processes, which results in—or even imposes—an increased readiness to organize communal coexistence. Numerous urban community gardens can be lumped into the same category, along with other formalized initiatives of community engagement via living, cultural, and educational projects. This category could also include non-formalized collective housing or park occupations, and spontaneous settlements or protest camps, which are similar to historical forms of commons. Understood as *particular commons*, embedded in the urban landscape and simultaneously cut from the same cloth, they form potential "third spaces"[9] that repeatedly escape the categories of private and public for brief moments.

The conditions for the development of these commons-like spaces seem to be comparatively prevalent in Berlin. The results of neo-liberal economic logic are felt widely, and yet the processes seem to be running askew. The city's once-island-like situation, combined with its spatial and structural diversity, porosity, cultural inheritance of a very strong activist movement, and proportionately high migrant population, creates physical, cultural, and social requirements for different levels of action. A generation that is artistically and creatively active, culturally active, and often living precariously also seems to have recognized that there is a shortage of affordable apartments and available free space, and sees the intensifying gentrification processes as a fertile climate for adopting a common property approach to urban spaces. On the other hand, they seem to be threatened by displacement and loss of livelihood, and express this through a headlong flight toward tangible involvement in the conditions of production of urban space. Berlin's heterogeneous urban fabric, perforated by a diversity of fallow land, seems to make it easier for collective organization to occur than it does elsewhere, and so practices are set in motion that can be interpreted as commoning in the broadest sense. Places emerge, then are taken over, managed, and maintained by various groups as subspaces of the city—as resources—many of them through horticultural work and expertise. But places of education and residence, and material and immaterial work, can also be interpreted as new or urban commons.

Berlin now has more than a hundred community gardens, all of which came to exist in the last decade. Most community gardens are set up as associations, which means a garden might be open to any interested party but is organized and maintained by a more or less established group. The same applies to the Rosenduft, an intercultural garden founded in the middle of a wasteland formed by a triangular railway junction called Gleisdreieck. With the help of a social agency, the initiators, along with refugees from the new Balkan states, fenced off a portion of the intentionally wild public park to create a place that contains both flower and vegetable gardens, and where people could exchange ideas and engage in productive work. By contrast, the Allmende-Kontor, established on Tempelhofer

Feld in 2011 and currently cultivated by five hundred members, is open to all park users and is legally covered by a temporary-use contract, so that it is only partially separated from the public sphere as a commons-type space. The most well-known urban community garden is probably the Prinzessinnengarten, described earlier, located on a former wasteland at Moritzplatz in Berlin. Run by people in the neighbourhood and other interested parties, it has been operating as a mobile urban farm since 2009. Legally secured as a not-for-profit limited liability company (GmbH), its organizational structure only partially resembles that of a commons, in that the decision-making powers are granted to only a few shareholders.

There are many more examples, but they all have in common an indistinct position between practising as an actual, community-supported commons and a privatized, rental, or social-agency-supported institution—on this basis, they aren't heterotopic places in the true sense of common land. Community gardening usually happens with landowners' uncertain terms of tolerance, takes place on utilitarian or peripheral areas, and must often accept the precarious status of provisional use. In addition, the participating gardeners are not always identified as actual commoners, and their numbers are subject to extreme fluctuations.

Given this, very few gardens can be accurately described as collectively supported, maintained, and cultivated commons. From among the multitude of commons-like practices, gardening takes on a special role as a direct link to the original form of commoning, and skilfully addresses the spatial conditions of the contemporary urban landscape. Gardening is an act of commoning that is reproductive, and a practice that builds community property to preserve the universal commons, to create specific commons in the first place, and, in the event of a failure to act, causes them to disappear.

The story behind the traditional commons is the history

of their dissolution via enclosures, particularly in the wake of their alleged original accumulation. The removal of the commons by, on the one hand, a so-called public, state-controlled economy and, on the other hand, privatization increasingly exploited by a market economy, also dismantled the commons as a social construct.[10] At the same time, in addition to the Berlin-based examples described here, the increasing number of theoretical papers addressing the commons demonstrates their strong position in the spectrum of societal interactions. Commoning processes are inherent elements of our living environment and become evident in every act of sharing, or every act that is collectively motivated and coordinated, from the collegial exchange of tools in the workplace[11] to the self-empowering occupation of a park.[12] Despite all attempts at appropriation, theories confirm a process of "ongoing commoning."[13]

And so the political image of the urban community garden also represents the relationship late-capitalist society, which is also socially and environmentally aware, has to nature, negotiation, and the fight for resources. This is characterized by displays of DIY and an aesthetics of scarcity, along with references to things growing wild and unplanned. The garden acknowledges its precarious status and nature's status as contested. And in this way, to a large extent, the garden has confirmed and established itself as described by Burckhardt in the occupied Basel City Garden: as spontaneous vegetation, as increasingly rare nature, as a farm, as a crisis, and as utopia. What at the time was apparent to only a few activists, well-meaning people, and aesthetics experts is now, nearly thirty years later, more obvious to experienced city dwellers. It's been incorporated into the repertoire of common design elements, and is practised in various types of gardens, from planting buffer zones to participatory parks planning. What, nevertheless, has emerged from the spectrum of urban community gardens is how they overlap with the commons on several levels: the negotiation, community, and resource conditionality of their existence, and their duality as a process and a product. They, too, as a subspace of a resource, must be managed collectively. Otherwise, they will dissolve. The act of commoning that occurs through gardening is both the labour and the yield.

The newly kindled discussion around common goods, as a result of increasing imbalances in resource distribution, has taken on a fruitful translation in the form of urban community gardens. This has brought forth a potent, albeit still unstable, type of common land within the urban garden. But only state and community protection of existing (spatial) resources as accessible and universal common property will make it possible to establish a new urban commons as a heterotopic, socialized component of the city's continuum beyond the public and the private. In the search to produce new forms of urban space, municipal and state administrations are indispensable partners, whose cooperation must be demanded if the experiment with common land spaces is to have a future.

However, of Burckhardt's series of images, the utopian image to describe community gardens seems weakest to date, which is why we'll return to the arbour in the Prinzessinnengarten at Moritzplatz, and its potential to form a third space. Erected between a small birch forest and a fence, clearly visible from the street, this three-storey, accessible wooden structure provides both a view of Moritzplatz, which is slowly being built up, and a view of its possible future. In a self-empowering gesture, the arbour, through its open, seemingly versatile construction, still appears as part of the garden, while the garden becomes a part of the arbour. The unclad wooden frame, which will eventually be covered, is waiting to be of use, and will gradually reinforce its role as a spatial structure. It is obvious that the structure is in transition from a resource-based state to a solid one. It is tantamount to an invitation. And it is now up to potential future commoners to recognize and develop this invitation.

If one sees the arbour in the Prinzessinnengarten as a commons in the making, its stable and initially immovable placement in the garden represents an experiment geared toward consolidation. The arbour rests on a strong foundation within the garden area. Through its sturdy, extremely oversized, and comprehensively assembled design, it communicates a promise of both expandability and constancy. In addition to this invitation to empowered commoners, the robust structure asks for a long-term legal contract to secure the land at Moritzplatz as a resource. A possible expansion of the definition of common land in the context of continued urbanization is epitomized in the arbour's static, three-dimensional spatial system. The commons, as a work in progress, could adopt the concept of a third space during the space-defining process and declare it an area for negotiation, in which self-governed commoners can take care of a commons-based space production with municipal protection. But for now, the arbour is above all else beautiful in the landscaped wilderness, visible from the street, and seemingly leaning against the fence, seeking to create a connection between the city, on the outside, and the garden, on the inside.

Dagmar Pelger is an architect and assistant professor in the Faculty of Urban Design and Urbanization at the Technische Universität Berlin, which is where her 2016 publication *Spatial Commons: Urban Open Spaces as a Resource* came to be. The key focus areas of her preoccupation with the production conditions of contemporary urban landscapes include critical cartography, design as a co-operative process, action-related creation of space, and the spatial exploration of urban common properties as spatial commons.

1   Lucius Burckhardt, "Nature Is invisible," in Why Is Landscape Beauti-
    ful? The Science of Strollology, trans. Jill Denton, ed. Markus Ritter,
    Martin Schmitz (Basel: Birkhäuser Verlag, 2006).

2   Lucius Burckhardt, "Wasteland as Context. Is There Any Such Thing as
    the Postmodern Landscape?" in Why is Landscape Beautiful?

3   Lucius Burckhardt, "Nature Is Invisible," in Why Is Landscape Beautiful?

4   Lucius Burckhardt, "Wasteland as Context. Is There Any Such Thing as
    The Postmodern Landscape?" in Why Is Landscape Beautiful?

5   Michael Koechlin, Die alte Stadtgärtnerei Basel, film documentary, 43
    minutes (Baden-Baden: Südwestfunk, 1988).

6   Lucius Burckhardt, "Nature Has Neither Cord Nor Outer Rind," in Why
    Is Landscape Beautiful?

7   Peter Linebaugh, The Magna Carta Manifesto: Liberties and Commons
    for All (Berkeley: University of California Press, 2008).

8   Lieven De Cauter, "Common Places: Preliminary Notes on the (Spatial)
    Commons," in DeWereldMorgen, October 14, 2013, https://www.
    dewereldmorgen.be/community/common-places-preliminary-
    notes-on-the-spatial-commons/

9   Ibid.

10 Silvia Federici, Caliban and the Witch: Women, the Body and Primitive
    Accumulation (New York: Autonomedia, 2004).

11 Michael Hardt and Antonio Negri, Common Wealth (Cambridge, MA:
    Belknap-Harvard, 2009).

12 Stavros Stavrides and Massimo de Angelis, "On the Commons. Beyond
    Markets or States: Commoning as Collective Practice" (public interview
    2009), in An Architektur (23) (Berlin: An Architektur e.V., 2010), 4–27,
    http://anarchitektur.org/aa23_commons/aa23_commons_heft.pdf

13 Peter Linebaugh, The Magna Carta Manifesto: Liberties and Commons
    for All (Berkeley: University of California Press, 2008).

SEVERIN HALDER

Learning by Digging—What You Can Learn from Community Gardening[1]

Sowing, watering, fertilizing, and harvesting are the key elements of gardening, but you learn much more than this in urban gardens, because they're a stage for different aspects of city living—like neighbourliness, urban ecology, food production, politics, and craftsmanship. The learning that happens on this stage forms a network of knowledge that links gardens to the diversity of life, practices, and communal visions. Various moments of exchange—whether through conversations, seeds, workshops, demonstrations, or recipes—form the nodes of this network. And the relationships that develop through interactions among community gardeners, neighbourhood initiatives, heads of lettuce, organic farmers, and compost worms are the channels along which this knowledge travels. Learning is a process that's deeply rooted in day-to-day practice; it isn't restricted to intellectual development but unfolds in the interplay between theory and practice. In urban gardens, learning by doing becomes learning by digging.

Even if the drive to garden varies greatly from person to person—it could be, for example, biographical, environmental, social, or pleasurable—urban community gardens form a particularly fertile environment for collective and creative learning. Shared experiences make it possible for adventurous learning communities to form and continuously educate themselves to grow their knowledge. Characteristic is the openness to making mistakes and to new forms of learning and teaching, where teachers and students willingly swap roles.

Because urban gardeners exchange knowledge through collective processes, we will now move to a conversation between garden activists, community gardeners, farmers, educators, and action researchers. This discussion is a meeting between so-called experts and those who like to refer to themselves—with their autodidactic learning—as dilettantes. In the process, the diversity and commonalities of urban gardeners and their educational practices emerge. And finally it becomes clear that urban gardens, even if they are part of a long tradition of gardening education, are now more than ever before both places where food is produced and places where people can learn about and experiment with creating a good life in the city.

Severin: What is the first thing that comes to mind when you think of education in urban gardens?

Frauke: People learn a lot in gardens without even realizing it. This goes without saying.

Gudrun: Urban gardens are places where you can try things out and learn practical skills, by watching, tasting, and touching.

Gerda: Urban gardens are places where learning takes place without someone standing there, a cane or pointer in hand; education happens collectively.

Joanna: The hierarchy of teaching and learning is dismantled, so that people of all sorts learn from one another. For example, adults learn from children.

Steffen: Raised beds, crooked paths, neighbourhood barbecues, and nice weather.

Severin: What role does education play in urban farming?

Joanna: It bothers me that education is such an abstract term, one that comes across as very academic—and education actually happens constantly, without a specified framework, through informal learning.

Roland: Education was the main reason we started the city garden. The urban part of it was important, too. But the farming definitely played a secondary role.

Gudrun: Urban farming? For me, urban gardens are part of urban farming. After all, outside of communal and personal gardens, there are also farmers who operate conventional farms in the city and who are not so open, and where other learning processes likely happen.

Frauke: We're talking about community gardens, so community action while planting.

Severin: Let's clarify the question of terminology. How do you feel about the term urban gardening? *What do you call what you do?*

Joanna: For me, *urban gardening* describes the phenomenon of the last few years that has been massively shaped by the Prinzessinnengarten and the rooftop gardens in New York, and of course doesn't take into account that there've been gardens in cities for a very long time.

Gudrun: For me, the term has become increasingly transparent. I think it's important that it's open, so as not to exclude anyone. I see it as encompassing more than community gardens; for me, it also includes allotment gardens, schoolyard gardens, therapy gardens, buffer zones, and all sorts of things. In our work, we have been using the term *community garden* with increasing frequency, because the term *urban* excludes smaller cities and rural municipalities. Even in these areas— for example, the Bavarian foothills of the Alps or the Black Forest—there are community gardens.

Steffen: I'm under the impression that most people who use the term *urban gardening* don't include allotment gardens. What do you think?

Sabine: Maybe for city dwellers the term *urban gardening* is what brought gardening out of the sleepy, narrow-minded allotment-garden corner. In the meantime, it seems to be merging. Here in Berlin, the garden colonies consult with the guerrilla gardeners[2] and they fight together to preserve garden plots and community gardens.

Gerda: For me, the term is more of a buzzword, used mainly by the media and wherever people are talking and writing about gardening in cities. I would describe it as city gardening using new and traditional methods.

Steffen: But what's also associated with the term, as opposed to other types of city gardening, is that you can basically call things into question, and criticize consumerism.

Gerda: For me, the broader concept of *urban gardening* is one that starts with the garden and leaves the various approaches open, whether it's social criticism or just putting your hands in the ground. What's exciting is the mixture, and that this gives rise to conversations about the variety of approaches. And another subversive point—whether the term *urban gardening* or *urban farming* is used depends on the promotional programs behind it.

Frauke: What's key here is what's happening on these sites, that social interaction is happening in a confined area, and attentiveness, diligence, and patience are being learned. So it doesn't really matter if it's called *urban farming* or *urban gardening.*

Severin: What do you think characterizes the learning processes in urban gardens?

Svenja: An important point is co-operative learning, and that everything is very much process-based. Otherwise, in universities and schools, a lot of value is placed on linear thinking. But, because so much can't be planned in a garden, you have to learn how to deal with processes, and that's a wonderful thing.

Joanna: I find the desire to learn very typical. Very different people come together, and they all want to learn, and they all want to learn different things.

Gerda: For me, the concept of education in gardens is very broad. It's about learning with all your senses, so not just with your head, but also your hands—and instinct, when totally different people do totally different things, is also part of it.

Steffen: I assume we all see learning as something that happens automatically by doing, in almost everything that we do—at least, when we do it together. However, this is more pronounced in urban gardens, because when it comes to gardening, lots of people just rush headlong into it without a concrete idea of what it is and how they can use it to change themselves and their environment in the process.

Severin: Can you share concrete examples? What have you learned from it?

Frauke: People just go ahead and do it, and learn while doing. The Allmende-Kontor on the Tempelhofer Feld is a great example. There are five thousand square metres, and you can do something here with the core idea of planting, but lots of other things also happen. This shows that if people have space and opportunities available to them, they want to do something with those opportunities. Then, in the process they learn all on their own, in part because the fears that often exist in formalized learning aren't present.

Gerda: Urbanized people learn that you can't garden according to a textbook or by pushing a button. You have to factor in the sun, wind, and mice.

Severin: Does anyone have a story that illustrates how learning happens in gardens?

Gerda: Well, urban gardens are chock full of stories, like the one about Vladimir from Kazakhstan—his tomatoes are always the biggest, even though his garden's conditions are highly unfavourable. Onlookers marvel at his sophisticated Kazakh planting techniques. And so the conservative middle-class from the outskirts of Berlin jealously eye Vladimir's fat, juicy tomatoes and see that things are not as they thought, and that someone from another country is not necessarily stupid.

Severin: How does this differ from formal educational processes?

Steffen: Formalized education works in such a way that you try to bring the same people together as often as possible, like in school, where things are sorted by age and supposed performance. If we assume that learning is a social process, naturally we benefit from diversity. The social differences are something that distinguish gardens from almost every other place of learning.

Gerda: I think it's like learning through a dialogue, whether with animals, plants, or other people. It's an open process without defined goals, and the challenge lies in finding a middle ground, a place where we can interact with one another so that we succeed.

Max: I've noticed that the relationship between humans and plants gives people an incredible amount when it comes to the meaningfulness of life. But also that plants reflect how well we take care of them and tend to their needs. These are processes that I believe are very beneficial to our society.

Gudrun: What's special is that you can try things out and make mistakes. That's how you learn that you can do something wrong.

Joanna: Well, every gardener, and that includes us, likes to say that making mistakes is allowed, but there are also perfectionist tendencies. So I think we should ask ourselves more frequently to what extent we're living up to the monumental ideals we try to emulate in the garden.

Max: I think that urban farming, when it's taught through formalized educational processes, is probably no longer what it was. This brings up the question of the value of a layperson's knowledge. The quote from the Allmende-Kontor—"We have to professionalize unprofessionalism"—comes to mind.

Severin: Where do you see gaps in the learning processes of urban gardeners?

Frauke: I see gaps when gardening becomes hip and stylish, like with the guerrilla gardening hype, which then leads to things being planted in a place where you can't take care of them, and then they die. The sense of purpose and attentiveness fall by the wayside when style is prioritized.

Sabine: When there are too many clashes between people with different convictions, and it isn't possible to moderate and bring them back to a common ground, there's often a huge gap.

Svenja: Gardening is a complex thing. It's quite often over-simplified in urban gardens, and then suddenly you have people proclaiming, "Hurrah—we're producing our own seeds and saving the world," instead of turning to people who have been doing this work for decades.

Max: Another problem is that you can't adopt individual professional farming methods without also adopting their implicit objectives. That's why we sometimes have to create new knowledge based on a combination of experience and expertise in urban gardens.

Steffen: For me, education is also a process that ideally leads to seeing yourself, and the world, differently. And there are many starting points in urban gardening, like land grabbing.[3] But if I look at this point, it might be a bit simplistic to say that education always happens when people come together, because it doesn't happen automatically, and has a lot to do with creating spaces for collective reflection.

Gudrun: Another question is how does what is learned stay in the garden and become common property? And how can we make this knowledge available to the garden network?

Joanna: There should also be space in gardens to reinvent the wheel, because when you've acquired the knowledge yourself, you have a different approach to using it.

Severin: Can you think of a particular situation that illustrates the knowledge gaps in urban gardens, like a beautiful urban garden scene full of amateurs?

Svenja: Well, in our garden, the beans were blooming, and suddenly, someone showed up wanting "those pretty orchids."

(*laughter*)

Joanna: What left quite an impression on me, even if it's really clichéd, was when we had a little boy in our garden who refused to believe me when I told him that this oval, orange thing was a tomato. Until we cut it up and ate it together.

Max: Another good one was when another allotment gardener came into our garden and was sent into a screaming rage by the sight of a dandelion blossom, and then gave us a long lecture about the danger of dandelions.

(*laughter*)

Max: Another thing we see a lot is people raking and weeding and maintaining things to the nth degree, but then they don't end up harvesting their vegetables. And then I realized that all they needed in order to make that final cut into the head of lettuce that had been cared for and nurtured for weeks on end was some company. Many people aren't used to seeing their plants as something they can use, probably because they're only accustomed to house plants.

Severin: For you, what are the political implications of education in urban gardens?

Svenja: I think it's very political to learn to take on responsibility. And that happens in these public spaces, where nothing happens if I do nothing, and where something definitely happens when I do something.

Frauke: Being actively involved in these processes changes our everyday actions. Like with our consumer behaviour, when we know how much effort goes into harvesting three carrots.

Steffen: I think we should always look critically at the concept of critical consumption, especially when people claim that's what they're doing, because if we look at discount stores, the market conformity of organic labelling, and the ongoing pressure on small-scale farmers... I would rather emphasize the aspect of change in cities. Gardening is an educational process that empowers us to act, and gives us the sense that we can create change. This in turn transforms, through a collective process, our image of how we "imagine cities," and can then result in transition town effects.[4]

Frauke: I'd also like to share a Rosa Rose example. A district parliament, likely without being completely aware of the impact of their actions, decided to post a pink plaque on the sidewalk to remind people that, thanks to police enforcement, private areas could no longer be accessed by the public. This was an acknowledgement of the commitment of city dwellers and their desire to allow the general public to make use of unused areas. The fact that this criticism of properties being parcelled into private lands was highlighted through the posting of a memorial plaque is rather special.

Gudrun: An example that illustrates the political side for me is a plant-dye workshop in the Mädchengarten (international girls' garden) in Gelsenkirchen. Some of the girls who take part attend special schools where chemistry isn't taught, and through learning how to use plant-based dyes, they obtain basic chemistry knowledge that they then go on to share in workshops at other schools.

Joanna: The whole garden is a political issue. I can't even break it down, even if for me the whole "right to a city" discussion is a key point. But as diversely political as gardens are, the education that happens in the gardens is also political.

Svenja: Whenever we create something with others who are different from us, when we create space, we have to deal with existing things, but we can also redefine many things. Learning this helps people mature and want to change things.

Severin: We have to draw our discussion to a close. Is there anything else you'd like to say?

Gudrun: Urban gardens and the various ways to learn in them, whether formally or informally, have not been properly recognized.

Gerda: I think everyone has a right to education. Educational opportunities for people are becoming increasingly diverse, so gardening in the city is an opportunity to connect people with educational opportunities and empower them to find their places in society. The concept of the undereducated class segregates society, and we are segmented in so many different ways, but here in the Allmende-Kontor we don't sort people; we include everyone, from those who can't read to university professors. And from there you can set other things in motion within the full range of urban society.

Steffen: I think you realize the garden can be a space that's about so much more, and where we can give thought to how we want to live. We could, however, improve our networking, to facilitate an even greater exchange of knowledge.

Severin: For me, this discussion makes it clear that gardens are a multi-functional platform for various topics, and learning processes form a sort of network that connects everything.

Thank you everyone, in particular for your energy, which has transformed the concept of this interview. Hopefully, this is just one of many more steps in the collective reflection on the urban garden movement.

DISCUSSION PARTNERS

Frauke Hehl has, for more than fifteen years, been providing support to self-management processes with, among others, workstation ideenwerkstatt e.V., which also includes collective gardens such as Rosa Rose and the Allmende-Kontor.

Gerda Münnich has been building networks for and providing consultation services to community gardens in Berlin for over ten years, in particular to intercultural gardens. She actively participates in, among others, the Allmende-Kontor and the Wuhlegarten.

Gudrun Walesch, as an employee of anstiftung & ertomis, provides consultation services and promotes and builds networks for community gardens across Germany.

Joanna Nogly is the co-founder of the Nuremberg city garden.

Max von Grafenstein is an organic farmer and founder of the Bauerngärten in Berlin.

Roland Brücher is the co-founder of the Nuremberg city garden.

Sabine Friedler is a founding member of the Bürgergartens Laskerwiese in Berlin and directs the neighbouring youth centre E-LOK, which includes active participation in community-based work.

Severin Halder is a garden activist in the Allmende-Kontor, an action researcher, and is doing her doctorate at the Freie Universität Berlin.

Steffen Kühne is working as an adviser for political education in the field of sustainability and social-ecological restructuring for the Rosa-Luxemburg-Stiftung.

Svenja Nette occupies herself with a multitude of things at the Prinzessinnengarten in Berlin.

Severin Halder is a geographer and enjoys gardening but has little time to do so, because he is busy mostly with self-organization, action research, political ecology, and emancipatory education.

1   The article is based on parts of the guide "Wissen wuchern lassen" [Let Knowledge Mushroom]. Severin Halder, Dörte Martens, Gerda Münnich, Andrea Lassalle, ed. Eckhard Schäfer, Wissen wuchern lassen—Ein Handbuch zum Lernen in urbanen Gärten [Let Knowledge Mushroom] Berlin: AG Spak., 2014), and the author's thesis, which is currently being written. The article was published under a creative commons licence.

2   David Tracey says, "Guerrilla gardening is autonomy in green. [...] You even get to define it for yourself." David Tracey, Guerrilla Gardening—A Manualfesto (Gabriola Island: New Society Publishers, 2007). "I call it 'gardening in public space with or without permission.'"

3   Land grabbing describes a process where land that was previously used by the local population is bought out by private or state investors or leased over extended periods.

4   Transition towns pose the question of how cities react to challenges and opportunities that arise through peak-oil and climate change.

Garden Shows as Driving Force—
The Staging of Urban Green Spaces

Private gardens and public parks are places of yearning and retreat. City dwellers in particular are driven by a desire to get away from the quick pace, the constant noise, and the smells of the city, and escape to a house with a garden on the outskirts of the city, or to an allotment plot.[1] We want to design a garden that meets our mind's eye, harvest our own food, and indulge in idleness.

Those who don't have a garden and can't leave the city can visit public parks and gardens. Today, parks—more or less well-maintained—are considered a natural part of the city and so far seem to be less affected by changes stemming from urban development. Yet many parks still find themselves transformed in keeping with the latest in garden and landscape design, and social developments, and thereby become both a mirror and showcase of their respective time.

Over the last few decades, many parks have been created or redesigned as part of garden shows. Garden shows, in turn, have developed into major events and an engine for urban development. Landscape architects and professional gardeners have the opportunity to put their skills to the test: the event site gets redesigned, exhibition buildings are erected. The latest plants are arranged in both indoor and outdoor pavilions, turf and flower-patterned carpets are rolled out, playgrounds are constructed, and high fences are installed around the site so admission can be charged. It often looks as though garden shows fit into a kind of modular principle—prepared for years, and over in a matter of days. But what actually remains after the event?

Garden shows have been subject to constant criticism in recent years. The costs to prepare and hold these events are high, creating feelings of resentment. Adding to that, the grounds are surrounded by a fence for the duration of the event, and no longer accessible to the local public. In order to recoup at least part of the cost, the price of admission is generally very high.

This was the case at the 2013 International Garden Show in Hamburg, which took place on the Elbe island of Wilhelmsburg. Further criticisms were that the park was intersected by a busy street, the advertising was inadequate, that it ended up in a financial deficit, and that there was property remaining afterwards that still had to be redeveloped into a park for everyday use. The great expectations that politicians placed on a garden show and an International Building Exhibition to transform and stabilize an entire city district, one that had up to then been regarded as marginalized, have yet to bear fruit.

This despite the fact that Hamburg stepped up to the plate, offering its long-standing tradition and experience. After all, the city had hosted six more or less successful horticultural exhibitions since the nineteenth century, and these made Planten un Blomen park the much-loved, centrally located destination for excursions that it is.

Looking Back

The first horticultural exhibitions took place in the nineteenth century. Exhibitions were generally seen as entertainment for the middle class. Thanks to garden shows, increasingly more large parks were created in the 1920s, like Essen's Grugapark in 1929. GRUGA stands for

Große Ruhrländische Gartenbau-Ausstellung (Great Ruhr Gardening Exhibition). The National Socialists organized three Reichsgartenschauen (Reich Garden Shows). From the largest—held in Stuttgart in 1939—the urban public park Höhenpark Killesberg emerged; it once again became the location for a garden show in 1950, and still exists. The introduction of national garden shows and international horticultural exhibitions after World War II were symbolic of the postwar rebuilding of cities. National garden shows have been held every two years since 1951, and the international horticultural exhibitions take place every ten years. In the past few years, regional garden shows have also made an appearance; most are organized by smaller cities. In the former German Democratic Republic, Erfurt became a permanent site for garden shows. Can garden shows therefore be considered a success story? What is it that such diverse cities—and, recently, regions—such as Hamburg (2013), the district of Havelland (2015), Eutin (2016), Berlin (2017), Bad Schwalbach (2018), Heilbronn (2019), and Erfurt (2021) are hoping to achieve with regional, national, and international garden shows? The association responsible for awarding and organizing national garden shows, the Deutsche Bundesgartenschau-Gesellschaft, has an answer at the ready:

> Garden shows represent the guiding principle behind "urban green spaces." They give rise to urban spaces where the young and the old, the long-established and the new arrivals, can gather, without exclusion. Their skilfully and creatively designed—with nature in mind—green spaces and urban biotopes are used for recreation, learning opportunities, and collective sport and leisure activities. They are intended for integration and thus play a decisive role in strengthening societal cohesion.[2]

This sounds like a good approach and the setting of high standards, but at the same time, one cannot help but suspect the involvement of solid economic interests.

It's true that many German cities are interested in hosting garden shows in order to rehabilitate existing parks and landscape fallow industrial or commercial areas. The event's aim is to attract tourists and improve the city's image. They not only target professional and hobbyist horticulturists, but also the general public. Playgrounds, high rope courses, and skate parks are included to attract families with kids. And when the garden show is over, there's the hope that the rehabilitated or newly created park will provide additional long-term value for the benefit of local residents.

The Example of Hamburg

As a historian, I am particularly interested in postwar garden shows, for their association with political and economic interests and incorporation of avant-garde architectural and artistic elements.

These aspects are apparent in the example of the city of Hamburg, which has hosted several garden shows since the nineteenth century. Following World War II, the city wanted to re-enter the international conversation by holding three international horticultural exhibitions.[3] These events had a significant impact on Hamburg's well-known park, Planten un Blomen, which, because of its beauty and central location, draws locals and tourists alike. A wander through the forty-seven-hectare park reveals different layers of time, topographical conditions, and changes in terms of urban development. It is worthwhile to follow the advice of sociologist Lucius Burckhardt, who, in the 1970s, coined the term *strollology*. He was a tireless advocate, wandering through urban spaces with open eyes, and asking: "Why is the landscape beautiful?"[4] Or asking instead: Why is the landscape the way it is? How did it get that way?

Before we start our walk, a look at the city map shows where we are: right near the former ramparts that once fortified the city. This wall featured twenty-two bastions and was erected around the city between 1616 and 1625. As in many other cities, the fortifications were torn down in the nineteenth century after the withdrawal of French occupiers, and the ramparts were redesigned as a public green area—a promenade—modelled on English landscaped gardens. And as early as 1821, the ten-hectare botanical garden was established as a scientific teaching garden near one of the former city gates, Dammtor.

Today's Planten un Blomen park, which includes the parks Große Wallanlagen, Kleine Wallanlagen, the Alter Botanischer Garten, and the original park, Planten un Blomen, was developed primarily for the purposes of horticultural exhibitions beginning in the nineteenth century. The first horticultural exhibitions took place in 1869 and 1897. Planten un Blomen was established for the Niederdeutsche Gartenschau 1935, a propaganda exhibition put on by the National Socialists. The low German name Planten un Blomen, which means "plants and flowers," is indicative that the park should have a predominantly North German character. The park's current configuration came about as a result of the international horticultural exhibitions that took place there in 1953, 1963, and 1973.

We'll begin our walk by approaching from the south. We've left behind the River Elbe, its jetties, and the hustle and bustle of tourists, and have hiked through the Alter Elbpark. It's likely that very few residents of Hamburg know that this park was the venue for Hamburg's first International Horticultural Exhibition in 1869, especially as nothing remains of the exhibition buildings or the garden itself. The thirty-four-metre-high Bismarck monument, a city landmark, was erected here in 1906. I am reminded of American-Canadian urban planning critic and activist Jane Jacobs and her descriptions of neighbourhood parks. In contrast to the large, popular parks, she characterized them as "dispirited city vacuums called parks, eaten around with decay, little used, unloved."[5] This is because the Alter Elbpark seems neglected and abandoned; parts of it even resemble a forest, and it's a gathering place for the homeless and others displaced from the nearby Reeperbahn, Hamburg's main red-light district. Hamburg politicians actually wanted to redesign the park in order to connect it to the ramparts for the 1973 International Horticultural Exhibition. Visitors would have no longer had to cross the busy Millerntordamm, a high-traffic street; instead, there would have been an underpass or bridge. As is often the case, however, a high price tag put an end to these plans. When Hamburg's application to host the 1973 International Horticultural Exhibition fell through after Munich won the bid instead, the plan was shelved.

We've now managed to cross the busy Millerntordamm, have left the Reeperbahn behind us to our left, and are entering the Großen Wallanlagen park, which is near the historic northern guardhouse, Millerntorwache. This park is landscaped with pathways, bodies of water, and a diverse selection of plants. It was the venue for the 1897 General Horticultural Exhibition. Exhibition halls, a greenhouse, cafés, and beer gardens were erected around the city moat, over which hung a suspension bridge. This was the first horticultural exhibition ever in Germany for which grounds were meticulously designed over the course of six months.[6] Today, nothing remains of the buildings and the topography. The buildings were torn down after the exhibition and the grounds were hit by air raids during World War II. After 1945, the former city moat was filled with rubble and the grounds were sculpted into a flowing, undulating landscape. Only one large building remains from the period before World War II—the Hamburg Museum (Museum für Hamburgische Geschichte), which opened in 1922 in the southeastern end of the park.

The filled-in city moat was to be made visible again for the 1963 International Horticultural Exhibition—not restored, but in a more abstract way, by channelling water through various pools, cascading waterfalls, and fountains. And in the process, a new building material was introduced to the park: concrete! The visitors of the time likely found the design rather bleak and bare, especially those who rode the gondola, which travelled from the Heiligengeistfeld through the Große Wallanlagen and Kleine Wallanlagen parks to the Alter Botanischer Garten. The overall impression was dominated by great expanses of lawn, water, and concrete. Critics' comments were predominantly positive, as the charming design elements of the 1950s were no longer popular.[7] In 1970s vernacular, however, Planten un Blomen was dubbed Platten und Beton (Slabs and Concrete), as the wide, paved paths of the 1963 and 1973 International Horticultural Exhibitions hardly appeared natural.

Even though the wide swaths of asphalt were scaled back in the 1980s, traces of the past's inhospitableness remain in certain areas: for example, in the wide, dark street underpasses at Sievekingplatz and Jungiusstraße. Here, the park grounds were lowered so that visitors to the park no longer had to cross the streets. The skating rink looks as though it was beamed in from elsewhere, its paved surface exposed and bare in the summer. There are plans to refurbish the skating rink in the years to come. The hope is that the site, which still retains its 1970s charm, and which, along with the entire park, is under heritage conservation, will not be completely transformed.

Otherwise, the formerly bare areas have really grown in, especially around the Teehaus, which is modelled after a Japanese tea house. This small, modern construction, built in 1963, appears to float over the pond where it is located. It is slated to be refurbished in the next few years, in accordance with its original plans.

The Mittelmeerterrassen, a series of south-facing terraces with Mediterranean flair, look like an oasis; they are located in the Alter Botanischer Garten. The striking white wooden chairs found here are a great place to soak up the sun. Our gaze wanders over the city's former moat, the condition of which is similar here to what it was before the dismantling of the ramparts. The terraces are formed by slate slabs, which store the heat and thus provide the perfect climate for hibiscus, cypress, and lime trees. The public greenhouses, which boast subtropical plants, cacti, and ferns, were designed by Hamburg architect Bernhard Hermkes and were not installed without protest. Critics were concerned that the complex would appear out of place in the Alter Botanischer Garten. The greenhouses still belong to the Botanisches Institut (Botanical Institute), which moved to Klein Flottbek in the late 1970s, where the Neue Botanische Garten was built.

Now we are approaching the area that was originally called Planten un Blomen. This is where the Zoologischer Garten opened in 1861—it's a zoo featuring elephants, monkeys, flamingos, and other exotic and native animals. It became less popular when the Tierpark Hagenbeck, a zoo in Stellingen, opened in 1907; this one was much larger and housed a wider variety of animals. The situation was seen as completely inadequate, until the National Socialists started a new prestigious project: in 1934, work began on the Niederdeutsche Gartenschau (the Low German Garden Show). Under the Reich Labour Service, 1,800 men began digging up the grounds. Although the park was initially to be dedicated to northern German flora, many exotic plants could be found in the mix: orchids, banana trees, cacti. As the "gateway to the world," Hamburg's park also had to exude an international character.

In 1953—a mere eight years after the end of World War II—Hamburg once again put itself in the spotlight with the Olympiade der Gärtner (Gardener Olympics), as promotion for the International Horticultural Exhibition. Germany was to present itself as a nation of peace-loving gardeners in front of a blooming backdrop. Fifteen nations participated; ten years later, this number climbed to thirty-five. In 1953, the park was transformed into a Mediterranean-inspired park, with palm trees, a Venetian gondola, and the Taverna Isola Bella, which served Chianti and espresso. After World War II and the years of scarcity immediately thereafter, the blooming gardens were particularly impressive. Scattered throughout the park were new cafés and modern works of art, and the Philipsturm, a tower boasting a viewing platform. Little was changed for the 1963 International Horticultural Exhibition, but in 1970, the path was cleared for new developments, because the city was set to host the 1973 International Horticultural Exhibition. This spelled an end for relics from the Niederdeutsche Gartenschau, including the entrance building, the cacti houses, and Orchideencafé. Buildings from the International Horticultural Exhibition that were less than twenty years old were also torn down in 1953: the Philipsturm, the Pflanzenschauhaus, and the Hamburg-Pavillon. Characterized by their light and modern appearance, these buildings—just like Café Seeterrassen, which still stands today—were designed by the architects who defined Hamburg's cityscape at the time.

Now building was happening on a much grander scale: the Congress Center Hamburg (CCH) and the 108-metre tall Plaza Hotel were constructed. With this complex, Hamburg wanted to make an international name for itself as a trade show and convention city. A covered path, built in 1990, connects the CCH to the nearby convention grounds. From this path, we can step into various sceneries. On the right, we can visit a Japanese garden, established in 1990; it features a rock landscape, a pond, and a thatch-roofed tea house set on a small island. On the left, we can step through an opening in the wall and onto a paved path running parallel to the one we're leaving. Beyond that is the wide Marseiller Straße, a sunken road that leads to the CCH basement. This could be filled in anytime, to gain a bit more park. It would compensate for the fact that adjacent areas of the park have been built up as a result of the current renovations to the CCH. Furthermore, the architectural competition's winning design envisions a better link between the park and the Dag-Hammarskjöld-Platz, which is behind the Dammtorbahnhof, one of Hamburg's four long-distance train stations.[8] Whether this expansion can take place once again depends on funding opportunities.

A few steps further to the right, and the scenery is once again completely different: on warm summer days, countless children can be found romping around in the playground, which was erected for the 1973 International Horticultural Exhibition. The yellow climbing mountains that children can crawl into, and that are equipped with long slides, are a key attraction. There are also wading pools and splash pads and all sorts of other climbing structures, see-saws, swings, and carousels.

There's a lively atmosphere in the park around sunset, when the water and light concerts begin. They've remained unchanged for years: fountains illuminated in an array of colours shoot up in time with the music that plays over loudspeakers. It's mostly catchy classical music, but sometimes it's a movie soundtrack. The first fountain, which came from a 1937 propaganda exhibition called Schaffendes Volk (Working People) in Düsseldorf, was installed in 1938.

This area has probably undergone the least amount of transformation. The lake has always been the heart of this park, and an attraction for park visitors. The range of the visitors to the park is always astounding, and today is no exception. This free, outdoor meeting place is probably the best location in Hamburg to experience the city's diversity.

On our tour, we've seen many artifacts from different decades. The horticultural exhibitions introduced many innovative design ideas and buildings, some of which still visibly exist. Some elements have more retro charm than others, but not all of them can be allocated to a specific decade at first glance. It is the plants that link the various areas and bring them together as a harmonious whole. Incidentally, Planten un Blomen is still Hamburg's best-maintained park, even if its budget hasn't increased in years. However, few people know about the tradition of horticultural exhibitions or the history of the ramparts.

And What Remains?

Nowadays, public parks and gardens are a facet of a rich and varied urban life. Gone are the days of strolling along pathways, stopping but never straying from them to gaze in contemplation at the plant world; instead, the green spaces increasingly open themselves up to us, drawing us in to engage in a wide array of activities. The phenomenon of Besitzergreifung des Rasens (taking possession of the grass) is a recent one. I like this slogan, coined by landscape architect Günther Grzimek—who designed the Munich Olympic Park in 1972 and renounced the representative roles of parks—because it's so descriptive: sunbathing, picnics, playing ball—we can do all these things now, because there are no longer any *Keep Off the Grass* signs.[9]

Public parks or gardens benefit from visitors because they fill these spaces with life. Whether a park that was created or redesigned because of a garden show is actually successful will only be revealed once the exhibition is over. What's key is that governments provide the funds and employees necessary for everyday use and for attracting visitors. Ultimately, we can only hope that the park's character will gain further shape based on the influence of its visitors.

Kristina Vagt is a free historian, author, and curator. Within the scope of her dissertation, she studied horticultural exhibitions from a historical standpoint. She likes stopping by Planten un Blomen, because there's always something new to discover, and she enjoys watching the visitors.

1   In the past years, some deeply personal books described this yearning—at times, self-deprecating, as is the case with Wladimir Kaminer—and became bestsellers: Wladimir Kaminer, Mein Leben im Schrebergarten [My Life in an Allotment Garden] (Munich: Goldmann Verlag, 2007) and Wladimir Kaminer, Diesseits von Eden. Neues aus dem Garten [This Side of Eden. The Latest from the Garden] (Munich: Goldmann Verlag, 2013); Jakob Augstein, Die Tage des Gärtners. Vom Glück, im Freien zu sein [The Days of a Gardener: The Joy of Being Outside] (Munich: Deutscher Taschenbuch Verlag, 2013).

2   Position paper of the Deutsche Bundesgartenschau Gesellschaft (German National Garden Show Association) for a white paper for the Federal Ministry of the Environment, Nature Conservation and Nuclear Safety, www.bundesgartenschau.de/ueber-die-dbg/unsere-aufgaben-und-ziele.html.

3   Kristina Vagt, Politik durch die Blume. Gartenbauausstellungen in Hamburg und Erfurt im Kalten Krieg (1950–1974) [Politics through Flowers. Horticultural Shows in Hamburg and Erfurt during the Cold War (1950–1974)] in Forum Zeitgeschichte (24) (Munich, Hamburg: Dölling & Galitz Verlag, 2013).

4   Lucius Burckhardt, Why Is Landscape Beautiful? The Science of Strollology, trans. Jill Denton, ed. Markus Ritter, Martin Schmitz (Berlin: Martin Schmitz Verlag, 2006). The fact that Burckhardt's research approaches remain current today and are also adopted by landscape architects can be found here: Günther Vogt, Landscape as a Cabinet of Curiosities. In Search of a Position, ed. Rebecca Bornhauser, Thomas Kissling (Zurich: Lars Müller Publishers, 2014).

5   Jane Jacobs, The Death and Life of Great American Cities (New York: Random House, 1961), 89–90.

6   Anne Steinmeister, Im Weltgarten zu Hamburg. Die internationalen Hamburger Gartenbauausstellungen des 19. Jahrhunderts. Ein Beitrag zur Entwicklung des gartenkulturellen Ausstellungs- und Kongresswesens in Deutschland [In the Hamburg World Gardens. The Hamburg International Horticultural Exhibition of the 19th Century. A Paper on the Development of the Garden Culture Exhibition and Congress Business in Germany] (Munich: Akademische Verlagsgemeinschaft, 2014).

7 Ulrich Conrads, "Hamburgs neuer Stadtgarten" [Hamburg's New City Garden], in Bauwelt (54) (Brauschweig/Wiesbaden: Friedr. Vieweg & Sohn Verlagsgesellschaft mbH, 1988), 62-63.

8 The competition's winning design is by POLA Landschaftsarchitekten, Berlin, www.pola-berlin.de/planten.html.

9 Günther Grzimek, Die Besitzergreifung des Rasens. Folgerungen aus dem Modell Süd-Isar [Taking Possession of Lawns: Consequences of the Süd-Isar Model] (Munich: Callwey, 1983).

Let It Grow

Late spring. I've been waiting forever for the weather to no longer feel wintry. I want to put seeds in little pots and place them in my IKEA greenhouse. It looks like a glass dollhouse and even has bunting. As I put it out on my tidy balcony in the spring sun, I think about the edible flower seeds or the future dried beans I'll be cooking, which I'll be starting in the greenhouse in plastic cups.

My plants don't take up much space; they're confined to my apartment. I don't dig up wild gardens, nor do I build raised beds on traffic islands. I wonder if this is typically female behaviour, and whether as a feminist I should reproach myself for the apolitical escapism of my rather kitschy plant escapades.

Why do I like to fill pots with soil? What role does (my) gender actually play in gardening? How many men fill cute little IKEA greenhouses with plants? Maybe the whole thing is not so apolitical after all? Everything grows, even my questions.

Race, Class, and Gender in One Garden

Looking at how gender—that is, so-called *social gender*—affects gardening doesn't just mean looking at how women garden; after all, men also belong to a socially constructed gender that didn't just fall from the sky. Here, though, I want to focus my microscope on women's gardens. On the one hand, the state of research on gender representation is somewhat clearer there, and on the other, there are exciting stories to tell, as women contrast with the supposedly neutral, or male, norm, poised in a luminous field between invisibility and divergence. In this context, use of the term *garden* refers particularly to a *private garden*, whether it's a backyard garden or allotment garden, a city garden or simple balcony garden. But looking at how gender affects gardening is not about lapsing into stereotypical traps, like women plant flowers, men plant trees—if they aren't uprooting them. Or women plant flowers, men barbecue. It means distancing oneself from normative "men are like this, women are like that" thinking, so we can gain a better understanding of how gender works, and how it's negotiated.

When I was little, I tried to plant things, to care for plants a few times, but I always failed. *I don't have a green thumb*, I thought to myself. You either have one or you don't. I never questioned it, assumed it was a birthright; if you have one, your plants magically never die. Now, I've been maintaining a green, flowering balcony garden for five years, and my efforts are increasingly met with success. I keep unreliable notes of what I've tried to grow, but I learn mostly through the plants I live with, discovering the conditions they need to thrive. I didn't grow a green thumb overnight. I just learned more.

Gender is similar, in that most of it is learned. We watch others, copy them, try things out. First of all, gender is very much accidental and ascribed, a category you might fit into or adapt to, but one that you have to somehow deal with, no matter what. The question of the extent to which we can live as the gender attributed to us arises: if we feel completely at home in the gender assigned to us at birth, how difficult is it to conform to stereotypes, or to not conform at all? In any case, the prevailing binaries do not do justice to a large diversity of gender identities that extend beyond the scope of the opposing male and female genders. Green thumb, yes or no, that's too simple, too binary; there are quite a few gradations between the two, just as there are for gender. Neither a green thumb nor gender differences, for example, in the form of abilities or weaknesses, are natural or just there. They arise through social conditions, prerequisites, opportunities, constraints, and demands. And so, just as the statement "I simply don't have a green thumb" confirms that one belongs to a category with certain attributed skills (or their absence) like a self-fulfilling prophecy, belonging to a gender is also practised and performed through similar evocations ("What we need now is a strong man," "Girls don't do math," "Children belong with their mother").

In any case, it's not as if gender categories are irrelevant or without effect on the topic of gardens. Research literature that addresses the different ways men and women garden posits that women tend to practise more subsistence gardening. If their income is insufficient, they provide for their families through gardening; they use less chemicals and pesticides, place more value on environmental impact and sustainability, are more likely to compost, and yet have smaller gardens than men. Studies from Kenya, Great Britain, and the Iberian Peninsula suggest that men play a bigger role when it comes to selling a garden's yield—for example, by choosing seeds that bear fruit that can be sold for higher prices.[1] This doesn't mean that we can draw conclusions about other gardeners, but it can at least provide a basis for interpreting these tendencies. Gender plays a major role in deciding who acts in the public and private spheres, who is the primary wage earner, or who is responsible for the family's welfare.

When I was little, maybe in primary school, I'd occasionally purchase seeds from the local department store. They were displayed in front of the store every spring and were pretty much the cheapest thing you could buy. I remember a packet of radish seeds the most: I took them home and buried them in our apartment building's courtyard. We had a balcony, but it would never have occurred to me to just ask for a pot and some soil. The dirt in the yard was probably fine for trees and grass, but otherwise it was very dry. I thought to myself: *Seeds, soil, what else do I need? Soon I'll be able to harvest them!* And so I harvested the radishes. Way too early. I was too curious about how it worked, and so I kept digging up my still-growing radishes. They didn't have the chance to become much more than thick, white, stringy roots before I pulled them up and ate them.

Not all people who would like to garden have equal opportunity to do so. It takes space and resources, and the power or ability to obtain space and resources. These things are not distributed unequally by chance, but primarily on the basis of various socially constructed categories, of which gender is only one. Others include race and class, age, being disabled/able-bodied, or level of education. These categories don't stand alone; they are directly linked to one another. Seeing them as interconnected is a concept called intersectionality.[2] Here, these categories and their often-associated discriminations are not simply combined; the situation of people who find themselves at a junction of different categories is also analyzed. For example, different expectations are placed on an upper-class white woman with respect to gardening than on a nineteenth-century, working-class white woman, or on a Black woman in a contemporary city. This is also linked to the phenomenon of constitution and accessibility issues, which go well beyond money or restrictions. Gender alone, therefore, cannot explain why people garden the way they do.

A Garden for Nobody But Yourself?

It's not as though I never came into contact with gardens. One of my grandmothers had a big garden with all kinds of plants on her property. As a child, however, I was only interested in the strawberries and the row of currant shrubs at the end of the garden. I could pick as much as I wanted. As for the rest, I was allowed to help with the watering, but otherwise, the same rules as those pertaining to my grandmother's dollhouse applied: it wasn't a place to play, to make a mess or to experiment. It was *her* garden. Otherwise, I saw gardens as belonging primarily to fathers, namely in the form of allotment gardens used as venues for children's birthdays, and so they functioned more as places dominated by men. A quick look at the websites of small garden associations further supports this: their boards consist mostly of (older, white) men, and for the most part, the positions of secretary or treasurer are mostly held by women (also white). Which also says little about who actually does what work in a garden.

In *A Room of One's Own*, Virginia Woolf writes that you need your own room and your own money in order to write. In order to garden, you also need the appropriate space and money, and at least a few aids. Tools, for example. And expertise.

Historically, land ownership is not a given, even for (married) well-to-do women, and they had to work to gain access to botany. This was made possible in part through gardening literature,[3] in which knowledge about plants was combined with descriptions of how women were expected to behave, often interspersed with allegories in which flowers were personified as women, illustrating virtues to be acquired or upheld. Rich women who had the opportunity to design their own garden according to their own ideas, moved within fixed gender norms, but they also changed them in the process.[4] Here, unlike for working women, the distinction between the public and private/domestic spheres played a much larger practical and symbolic role. Gardens managed by women became an interface between the private and the public. This made it possible, within the context of respectable femininity, to acquire expertise and professionalism, build networks with other women, and get involved, for example, in gardening clubs, to conduct trades with students at horticultural shows, and gain public recognition.[5]

Even now, gardens can be an interface between private and public spaces. Women who are involved in community gardens in large North American cities, for example, report that these gardens offer girls and young women safe spaces outside of the home and an opportunity to take part in public life without harassment.[6]

The Garden Gate Is Open

I have since grown up, and now I have money to purchase my own ingredients for my (balcony) garden, like my green-house. I have access to the internet, and I can quickly research what I need. On one foray, I put my child in the stroller and head to the local hardware store to purchase soil and other materials. I attempt to push the stroller, loaded with a forty-litre bag of soil, to the streetcar, which is quite a struggle. But then some dear neighbours approach me in the parking lot. They load my soil into their car and drive it home for me, and suddenly I'm not as sweaty. These same neighbours have already picked up big pots for my balcony. My seedlings will sprout properly, my radishes will thrive in the rich soil, and everything has enough space to grow. I reach the understanding that gardening has a lot to do with sharing and depending on the help of others. And I'm happy to share my radishes.

I take part in an online seed exchange and receive seeds in the mail; all I know about them is what type of care they require. I have no idea what they will grow into. Another online source, one that might have a similar function as garden advice columns for women in the eighteenth and nineteenth centuries, is Pinterest. Embedded amongst instructions on homemaking, I find many well-presented tips on how to grow plants. Gardening is also a lifestyle here. In place of garden advice columns, which encouraged women to be virtuous while gardening, we now have lifestyle magazines and blogs, which awaken consumer desires. Even guerrilla gardening is adapted to fit this framework, with seed bombs shaped like hand grenades on offer in the non-food sections of bookstores, or DIY versions that you can gift to friends. These seed bombs are not tossed over construction fences onto abandoned city lots with the intent (or with the commitment) of creating a community garden, like the one in the heart of Loisaida, in New York City.[7] They are more likely to be planted directly in private balcony gardens, and serve more to embellish private spaces than as tools to reclaim public spaces.

With respect to beauty and gender representation, at first glance, gardening offers a great deal of potential. You get dirty while gardening, you don't have to look nice while gardening, it's okay to get sweaty and dig through the earth until your fingernails are black. This despite the fact that ads for garden tools and accessories give a totally different impression, depending on the gender being targeted. They advertise products designed to make women look good even while digging up dirt, like delicate garden shears and flowered gloves for tender hands, whereas products for men appeal to values like strength and skill. And at the same time, high-powered gardening devices are depicted as toys to appeal to the child in the man.

As for gardening and the topic of beauty, things are more complicated. Women-as-flowers not only play a role in centuries-old allegories, but the embodiment of women as silent, decorative elements still occurs today, as does the depiction— or rather, shameful covering—of the vulva/vagina by flowers. This becomes particularly evident when we look at the use of stock photos on the websites of clinics offering intimate cosmetic surgery.[8] The naked female body is displayed in a public place and is treated as a public space to be altered, on which nothing should grow wild—everything should be smooth, finely trimmed. This is a supposedly natural state that operates in the same way as natural parks, which present the illusion of untouched vegetation, rather than the domesticated and civilized.

With regard to physical norms for women, the triad of race, class, and gender plays a particularly significant role; especially when the issue of race comes into play, different gender-related beauty ideals are further amplified. Wild, unruly hair and naturalness are not only assessed differently when it comes to men and women, but even moreso in the demands placed on Black women to straighten and lighten their hair. This is about yielding to white beauty standards and adapting to distinctions of class in order to be accepted in the professional world, and so as to not be categorized as *wild*. Bodies that are labelled as *wild* draw a parallel to the wild countryside that, through gardening and landscaping, becomes *civilized*. Gardening is symbolically, as well as concretely through the cultivation of occupied land, closely linked with colonialism.

Work? What Work?

But what kind of work is gardening, and for whom and by whom is it done? There is already a lot of research on the division of work among opposite-sex couples. The gardening work discussed there tends to be leisure or hobby gardening and can be characterized by the catchphrase "misrepresentation of labour as leisure." With gardening, this comes into play because women do the majority of caregiving work and therefore have less leisure time than men, so gardening is wrongly considered free time.

And yet it cannot be ignored that gardening is also caregiving, in three respects. First, for the plants, which need to be tended. Second, for the gardener; this self-care makes it possible to take time for yourself, in nature, in which you can create your own space. And third, it is caring for others, which includes providing them with the fruits of your labour, and also to create a space for them to relax. Of course, one might ask to what extent gardening for self-care is not escapism of sorts, and ties up energy that could be spent on other work. On the other hand, a garden, if it can be used as a place for recreation, can be a place through which resistance again becomes possible, and where solidarity can be practised through sharing and collective work.[9] One example of a garden as a space for community and resistance can be found in the fictional prison garden featured in the television series *Orange Is the New Black*.[10] But even in the real world, many international community gardens provide their members with space to gather and organize outside of garden work, or the spaces themselves are created as a direct result of environmental activism.

A Fig Tree Full of Possibilities

And why am I actually doing this now? I don't find flowers exciting, but I love getting something to grow, and to see how a little seed can grow into a towering pole bean. I want to enjoy the fruits of my labour, to nibble away at them. And I like the idea that by keeping a garden, however small it may be, I'm not alone in the world, but connected to it, obliged toward it.

At the end of the summer, I was given a key to an allotment garden. It's not my own; friends of mine happened to hear that I wanted to work in a garden and they'd been looking for people to share the garden for a long time, because it requires a lot of work. Now we're making plans for spring. At the end of August, I was able to plant a few rows of corn salad and yes, even radishes; I was able to do some raking, help with the potato harvest, and snack on the ripe figs (not without thinking of Sylvia Plath, in whose novel, *The Bell Jar*, metaphorical figs hanging from a tree represent all of life's opportunities, which rot away if you can't decide which fruit to eat). I'm learning skills like pruning grape vines, and enjoying how wild and overgrown the garden is, and how much is waiting to be discovered in the shade. My plants, which have outgrown the mini IKEA greenhouse on my windowsill, now have a place to continue growing. The mystery plant from the online seed exchange ended up being a hollyhock, and it has also been transplanted into the new garden. I'm looking forward to being able to grow all kinds of edible things from tiny seeds, like delicious currant tomatoes, whose seeds I extracted by sucking on the tender fruit, which will grow into tall vines. And most of all, I'm looking forward to how our friendship will grow as we work together, share with one another, create a beautiful space, and celebrate holidays together, while reaping what we sow.

Nicole von Horst studied creative writing in Hildesheim and is now studying American studies and sociology, majoring in gender studies, in Frankfurt am Main. In 2013, she was involved in creating the hashtag #aufschrei (translation: outcry), which led to a country-wide debate on the topic of everyday sexism, and is co-author of the #ausnahmslos (translation: without exception) manifesto against a racist appropriation of the fight against sexual violence. She writes regularly for the online magazine kleinerdrei.org and is not only quite skilled when it comes to greenhouses, but also electric hedge shears.

1   R. R. Simiyu, "I Know How to Handle My Husband: Intra-household Decision Making and Urban Food Production in Kenya, Eastern Africa, " in Social Science Research Review, June 2015: 63–81.
Susan Buckingham, "Women (Re)construct the Plot: The Regen(d)-eration of Urban Food Growing," in Area 37 (2), June 2005: 171–79.
Victoria Reyes-García, Sara Vila, Laura Aceituno-Mata, et. al., "Gendered Homegardens: A Study in Three Mountain Areas of the Iberian Peninsula," in Economic Botany 64, September 2010: 235–47.

2   The term and the concept were coined by Kimberlé Crenshaw, and explained in depth in her 1989 essay "Demarginalizing the Intersection of Race and Sex: A Black Feminist Critique of Antidiscrimination Doctrine, Feminist Theory and Antiracist Politics" in the University of Chicago Legal Forum and in 1991 in "Mapping the Margins: Intersectionality, Identity Politics, and Violence against Women of Color" in the Stanford Law Review.

3   Sarah Bilston, "Queens of the Garden: Victorian Women Gardeners and the Rise of the Gardening Advice Text," in Victorian Literature and Culture 36 (1) (Cambridge: Cambridge University Press, 2008) 1-19. http://www.jstor.org/stable/40347590.

4   Vera Norwood, Made from This Earth—American Women and Nature (Chapel Hill, NC: The University of North Carolina Press, 1993).

5   Glenn Moore, "'A Very Housewifely Ambition': Women Gardeners in Industrialising America," in Australasian Journal of American Studies 20 (1) (Auckland: Australian and New Zealand American Studies Association, 2001), 18-30. http://www.jstor.org/stable/41053839.

6   Monica M. White, "Sisters of the Soil: Urban Gardening as Resistance in Detroit," in Race/Ethnicity: Multidisciplinary Global Contexts 5, No. 1 (2011): 13-28. muse.jhu.edu/article/462927.

7   Karen Schmelzkopf, "Urban Community Gardens as Contested Space," in Geographical Review (July 1995): 364–81.

8   Anna-Katharina Meßmer, Überschüssiges Gewebe. Die weiblichen Genitalien zwischen Medikalisierung von Ästhetik und Ästhetisierung der Medizin [Excess Tissue. Female Genitalia Between the Medicalization of Aesthetics and the Aestheticization of Medicine] (Wiesbaden: Springer VS, 2017).

9 Monica M. White, "Sisters of the Soil: Urban Gardening as Resistance in Detroit," in Race/Ethnicity: Multidisciplinary Global Contexts 5 No. 1 (2011): 13-28. muse.jhu.edu/article/462927.

10 Orange Is the New Black is a Netflix series from 2013 that revolves around stories about female inmates in a New York State prison, based on the book Orange Is the New Black: My Year in a Women's Prison, by Piper·Kerman. The garden in the series is a greenhouse that some of the women appropriate, and it acts as a place they can retreat to, and where they can celebrate friendships and exert their power or influence. It's also a place where, for example, smuggled goods can be hidden or where a dead person is hidden in the area that later becomes a garden.

MAXIMILIAN PROBST

A Green Thumb Requires Your Whole Hand

Is the garden good? Are gardeners good? These simple questions, you'd think, would be easy to answer with an emphatic yes! Look closely at the history of civilization, and you can't help but get this impression. For example:

> When Idleness the garden gate
> Threw open wide, and unafraid
> To that sweet spot quick entry made.
> Then burst on my astonished eyes
> A dream—an Earthly Paradise.[1]

This was written in *The Romance of the Rose* in the thirteenth century. And regardless of where you turn from this point in time, whether back to the Old Testament, to the Garden of Eden, or the Song of Solomon, where the lover is allegorized as a garden; or to the gardens of Allah, in which fruits and dates and pomegranates (alongside "chaste maidens restraining their glances") await the faithful; or to the beautiful Islamic concept of death being represented by the return of the nightingale to the eternal rose garden; or eastward, where Zen monks gaze out beyond moss, water, and stones into the nothingness of enlightenment Buddha found while sitting under a fig tree; or to the not-so-distant past, to the great Bildungsroman of German literature, to the gardens and garden care in Goethe's *Elective Affinities*, Stifter's *Indian Summer*, and Thomas Bernhard's *Extinc-*

tion: the garden is always a symbol of an enclosed, holy, and healing area in which the human being, in accordance with generations of patriarchal history, is presented as a man who gets his money's worth.

Yes, the garden is what is good in this world, and gardeners are also good; it's as simple as that. But philosophy, and here one can agree with Martin Heidegger, is unfortunately not in the service of simplification. It is there to make life more difficult. And it seems to me that this is what philosophy has in common with the garden. Gardens, I propose, are a problem.

Up to this point, the garden hasn't been a problem for philosophy. On the contrary: often enough, its nature was presupposed. It's true that Socrates is primarily known as a marketplace philosopher, a philosopher of the *polis*, of public space, who spoke with everyone whose path crossed his. But his student, Plato, also urged Socrates to conduct his dialogues in quiet groves, or stretched out in the shade of a sycamore tree. Plato himself preferred to retreat from public places. He founded his well-known *Akademeia* before the city gates, and moved his lessons to his private garden, apparently to avoid the noise of Athenians' public green spaces. Epicurus later followed suit, except that his school of philosophy was housed in a spacious garden within the city walls. This development, which has continued to the present day, can be summarized as follows: the higher the walls that shield the thinker from their noisy surroundings, the more freely their thoughts flow. So maybe philosophers haven't explored the gardens as subjects because gardens are literally the ground on which they stand. But that's also a problem.

The first major garden controversy was a long time coming and is associated with the names John Locke and Jean-Jacques Rousseau. Locke, the English founding father of liberalism, maintained that the appropriation of nature through work legitimized the idea of private ownership. According to Locke, a fallen apple becomes the private property of the first person who makes the effort to pick it up off the ground.

Everyone who has children, and who has taken these children to a forest in search of wild mushrooms—or even just hunted for Easter eggs in a garden—knows this is not the best example. Because if someone calls out, "There!" and points to the apple in question, that person can then claim ownership on this find even if someone else is quicker to actually pick it up. So, does the effort of discovery—and this leads in a straight line to our modern-day copyright and patent laws—therefore trump the effort of execution?

Locke knew that his apple example was not sufficient. To his argument he added that it is the reclamation of land that legitimizes title of ownership. Fields and fruit belong to everyone. But as soon as someone cultivates a parcel of land, the harvest is the fruit of their labour, and therefore their property. Garden culture begins at this point. Marie-Luise Gothein, the most prominent garden historian in the German language, clearly describes this:

> Under primitive conditions, the cultivation and design of gardens could only begin when a wandering tribe found a place to settle. The nomad drove his herds across the unfenced pastures. When, however, with the aid of the pickaxe, he broke the ground for cultivation and a fixed dwelling place, he was compelled to erect a fence, in order to protect the homestead from enemies and wild beasts.[2]

From a historical perspective, putting a fence around a garden marks the start of private ownership. For Locke, this property was a gift from God, because God gave people the world in order to make them subservient. Humankind obeys God by transforming the wild into cultivated property, creating a garden world out of God's crude creation—this is the utopian content of Locke's idea. If, however, there was no concept of property, and no state as the agency for enforcement of ownership claims, then humans, according to Locke, wouldn't have even begun to transform the world into a garden, because they'd always have to reckon with the possibility that someone else might reap what they'd sown.

This is where Rousseau comes into play, and he simply turns everything postulated by poor Locke on its head. Angered, the Genevan philosopher wrote:

> The first man who, having fenced in a piece of land, said, "This is mine," and found people naïve enough to believe him, that man was the true founder of civil society. From how many crimes, wars, and murders, from how many horrors and misfortunes might not any one have saved mankind, by pulling up the stakes, or filling up the ditch, and crying to his fellows: Beware of listening to this impostor; you are undone if you once forget that the fruits of the earth belong to us all, and the earth itself to nobody.[3]

The enclosing of the garden unleashed power. It led to envy and resentment (even now, a majority of people still feels that the tomatoes in their neighbour's garden appear larger and redder than their own) and, by civilizing them, drives humans to ruin. Rousseau recapitulated, stating: "...property was introduced, work became indispensable, and vast forests became smiling fields, which man had to water with the sweat of his brow, and where slavery and misery were soon seen to germinate and grow up with the crops."[4]

This is stylistically brilliant and just as difficult to refute as Locke's praise of ownership. So the question is: now what? Is the garden a gift from God or the scourge of humankind? Or is there perhaps a middle ground? A society of gardeners who can make do without ownership?

The English statesman Thomas More conceptualized this idea in his book, *Utopia*, even before Locke and Rousseau addressed these concepts. He writes about the fictitious island of the same name:

> ...Every house has both a door to the street, and a back door to the garden. Their doors all have two leaves, which, as they are easily opened, so they shut of their own accord; and there being no property among them, every man may freely enter into any house whatsoever. At every ten years end they shift their house by lots. They cultivate their gardens with great care, so that they have both vines, fruits, herbs, and flowers in them; and all is so well ordered, and so finely kept, that I never saw gardens anywhere that were both so fruitful and so beautiful as theirs. And this humor of ordering their gardens so well is not only kept up by the pleasure they find in it, but also by an emulation between the inhabitants of the several streets, who vie with each other. And there is, indeed, nothing belonging to the whole town that is both more useful and more pleasant. So that he who founded the town, seems to have taken care of nothing more than of their gardens.[5]

The problem with More is that we don't really know what he's actually trying to say. The whole work is confusing: sometimes the life, and land, in Utopia seem like a dream, and at others, they seem like a nightmare; sometimes the text reads like an educated, political blueprint, but then this impression shifts, and More's entire undertaking seems like satire. More never disclosed the purpose of the gardens in *Utopia*. It is, however, clear what purpose they do not serve. The ideas we are familiar with nowadays of gardens being places to relax, and places of love (shady arbours!), find no parallel in More's work. He writes that in Utopia:

> There's never any excuse for idleness. There are also no wine-taverns, no ale-houses, no brothels, no opportunities for seduction, no secret meeting-places. Everyone has his eye on you, so you're practically forced to get on with your job, and make some proper use of your spare time.[6]

As for what's respectable, that's always decided by others. We can probably say that More's community gardens promise dubious pleasure; the happiness of the individual can only be found in the reflection of a totalitarian society.

Incidentally, the fundamental notions of utopia are no different; its promises of pleasure are also dubious. And these bring the sense of possibility to the world, which is undoubtedly a blessing: we will tackle things, change them, and we do not have to accept them as God-given or respond to everything with yes and amen, once we've imagined they can be different and better. But this is simultaneously a curse: thanks to the sense of possibility, we find ourselves heading directly toward optimizing everything and everyone, and are unlikely to find peace until everything has reached its optimum level— so never! And: "There might be something even better than what I already have"—let a husband try saying that to his wife!

Voltaire grappled with these thoughts, too. His philosophical fable, *Candide*, is a satirical rejection of Leibniz's thesis that the world in which we live is the best of all possible worlds (because if it is not, according to Leibniz, then God wouldn't have been working to the best of his abilities, and even if His ways are inscrutable, the idea that He might have botched creation seems virtually impossible). So Voltaire allows Candide to discover that the world in which he lives is the worst world imaginable, rotten from the ground up. The only route to happiness appears to be withdrawing into one's own garden, which one has to personally cultivate. With *Candide*'s "we must cultivate our garden," Voltaire takes the high-reaching utopian and revolutionary hopes of his epoch and scales them back to quiet, modest work in our immediate environment.

Today, Voltaire's local utopias are blooming like never before. After the transition from emancipation to reigns of terror and restoration played out often enough on the world's historical stage, the local utopia now seems like it's on the safe side. If you cultivate your own garden, you certainly can't go wrong, can you?

Unfortunately, yes! Unfortunately, this is also no sure thing; unfortunately, here, too, there is doubt. Because sometimes—according to Brecht—even talking about trees is almost a crime. Sometimes the world spirit calls us to centre stage, sometimes it is necessary for everyone to turn away from their garden and occupy themselves with nothing other than global causes, the utmost common good, in order to create conditions under which one can continue to care for one's own garden. And always, always, always, focusing on the local utopia runs the risk of degenerating into a small, enclosed corner of joy.

The cosmopolitan symbol for this exclusive happiness was the English landscape garden. Its principle is to look like a natural landscape with a certain amount of wild growth. At a time when England, thanks to huge coal reserves, was already on the path to becoming the world's first industrialized nation, English gardeners went to great lengths to make the cultivated appear natural, a departure from the previously fashionable French Baroque Gardens, which were only an extension of a house or castle's architecture into the outdoors. Therefore, in these gardens, the open landscape stretches as far as the eye can see. As though anyone could walk through it. As though the field blends seamlessly into the world around it, even while one cultivates and tends their own garden. This impression is due to the fact that there are no fences or walls to interrupt the gaze. Instead, deep ditches rim the property. Ditches—what makes them so pleasant (provided we find ourselves on the right side) is that we can always look past them.

There are plenty of these local utopias! The most famous is currently the flowering garden called Prenzlauer Berg in Berlin. Cosmopolitan, liberal, organic, social at its very heart—and cut off from the proletariat and migrants of the neighbouring district of Wedding by a deep ditch.

I have now quietly started using the garden as a metaphor. Voltaire appears to be doing this, too: Candide's garden has been read as a metaphor for the work of the scholar in his study. "Tending one's garden" has also been interpreted as Voltaire's nod to his friends Diderot and d'Alembert, who painstakingly tried to compile the knowledge of the world into their *Encyclopédie*. Gardening is the literary, almost endless, work of becoming enlightened.

Plato—to circle back—stretched the garden metaphor even further. In a dialogue with Phaedrus, he says Socrates described writing as a "garden of letters." Socrates does not mean this to be especially positive. For him, the "garden of letters" is a game, played for fun, justified particularly as a memory aid, as something for the old and senile. Those who are still in full possession of their faculties should, if at all possible, refrain from writing as much as possible, and should use direct discourse to obtain and disseminate knowledge from person to person. Writing, on the other hand, Socrates complains, rambles about everywhere, among the intelligent as well as those for whom it is meaningless: "...if they are maltreated or abused, they have no parent to protect them; and they cannot protect or defend themselves."[7]

The criticism of writing is now more topical than ever, in these times of social network stress and shitstorms, in these times of global decontextualization and disinhibition. But this doesn't change the fact that things were already much more complicated for Plato. After all, he personally wrote down Socrates's criticisms of writing and popularized it as a literary genre—the philosophical dialogue that introduces each statement into the game of interpretation. Jacques Derrida later deduced that writing, for Plato (though also not just for him), is both a gift and also a deadly substance, according to the double entendre of the German noun *gift*,[8] which stems from the Old High German verb for giving, but in modern-day usage translates to *poison*.

The same applies to the garden. It, too, is a poison—no matter which pesticides and insecticides are used in it today. The garden is a blessing and a plague, even in its everyday use. Who doesn't dream of spending a quiet summer day in their own garden, in the shade of a lilac shrub, and with the company of a good book? Is there anything nicer, more peaceful, anything closer to paradise? But anyone who has a garden knows that you spend very little time sitting in it; instead, you're often kneeling to pull out a weed here, to prune something back there. And what right do I have to speak of weeds here? What curious notion allows us to see the garden as a peaceful paradise, as good, if a garden can only come about because a large portion of the flora is mercilessly persecuted and kept under control?

Gardens are not all good. All gardens, whether English, French, or Japanese, resemble the fairy-tale garden described by the Brothers Grimm, "Where it was half summer and half winter. On the one side the most beautiful flowers were blossoming—large and small. On the other side everything was bare and covered with deep snow."[9] In other words: a green thumb requires your whole hand! Gardens are not healing, sacred spaces. They are utterly ambivalent.

But perhaps that is precisely wherein their purpose—and our salvation—lies. Our daily life, our modern society, is also hopelessly ambivalent. As participants in a market economy competing for scarce goods, we are supposed to sharpen our elbows; as citizens, we are supposed to reach out to our neighbours; as believers, we are supposed to turn the other cheek when we're slapped in the face. Or another example: the modern man! In the morning, he changes diapers, runs a consulting services company over lunch, has a colleague hanging on his every word at an after-work-party, and, in the little time he has for his wife at the end of the day, is filled with pride by his loyalty. In short: the buzzword *ambivalence* is about taking the whole of the modern age by the collar.

This ambivalence might seem unreasonable to some. But what can be considered a real impertinence to date is merely every socio-political attempt to return to old unambiguities or to invent new ones. The motto of modern-day Enlightenment might be: have the courage to face down the impertinence of an ambivalent modern age! Those who cultivate their own gardens are always doing just that.

Maximilian Probst is an editor for the German newspaper *Die Zeit*. Instead of gardening himself, he would rather have someone else do the gardening, so he can devote his time to books. Because he doesn't have the means to do this, he occasionally has to reach for his own hedge clippers. But what often begins feeling like a chore, he often ends up finding rather enjoyable.

1   Guillaume de Lorris, The Romance of the Rose, Volume 1, trans. Frederick Startridge Ellis (Letchworth: J. M. Dent and Company, 1900).

2   Marie-Luise Gothein, A History of Garden Art, trans. Laura Archer-Hind (Cambridge: Cambridge University Press, 2014).

3   Jean-Jacques Rousseau, Discourse on the Origin of Inequality, trans. Donald A. Cress (Indianapolis: Hackett Publishing Company, Inc., 1992).

4   Ibid.

5   Sir Thomas More, Utopia (New York: The Columbian Publishing Company, 1891).

6   Ibid.

7   Plato, Phaedrus, trans. Benjamin Jowett (360 BCE). http://classics.mit.edu/Plato/phaedrus.html

8   TN: The first letter of a German noun is always written in uppercase.

9   Jacob and Wilhelm Grimm, "The Summer and the Winter Garden," trans. Jack Zipes, in The Original Folk and Fairy Tales of the Brothers Grimm: The Complete First Edition (Princeton; Oxford: Princeton University Press), 225-27. doi:10.2307/j.ctt6wq18v.75.

INVISIBLE PUBLISHING produces fine Canadian literature for those who enjoy such things. As an independent, not-for-profit publisher, our work includes building communities that sustain and encourage engaging, literary, and current writing.

Invisible Publishing has been in operation for over a decade. We released our first fiction titles in the spring of 2007, and our catalogue has come to include works of graphic fiction and non-fiction, pop culture biographies, experimental poetry, and prose.

We are committed to publishing diverse voices and experiences. In acknowledging historical and systemic barriers, and the limits of our existing catalogue, we strongly encourage writers from LGBTQ2SIA+ communities, Indigenous writers, and writers of colour to submit their work.

Invisible Publishing is also home to the Bibliophonic series of music books and the Throwback series of CanLit reissues.

If you'd like to know more, please get in touch: info@invisiblepublishing.com